FAREWELL TO MANZANAR

Jeanne Wakatsuki Houston

EDITORIAL DIRECTOR Justin Kestler
EXECUTIVE EDITOR Ben Florman
DIRECTOR OF TECHNOLOGY Tammy Hepps

SERIES EDITORS John Crowther, Justin Kestler
MANAGING EDITOR Vince Janoski

WRITER Ross Douthat, Brian Phillips
EDITOR Boomie Aglietti, John Crowther

This edition published by Spark Publishing

Spark Publishing
A Division of SparkNotes LLC
120 Fifth Avenue, 8th Floor
New York, NY 10011

First edition.

Please submit all comments and questions or report errors to www.sparknotes.com/errors

Library of Congress Catalog-in-Publication Data available upon request

Printed and bound in the United States

ISBN 1-58663-831-9

Introduction:
Stopping to Buy SparkNotes on a Snowy Evening

Whose words these are you *think* you know.
Your paper's due tomorrow, though;
We're glad to see you stopping here
To get some help before you go.

Lost your course? You'll find it here.
Face tests and essays without fear.
Between the words, good grades at stake:
Get great results throughout the year.

Once school bells caused your heart to quake
As teachers circled each mistake.
Use SparkNotes and no longer weep,
Ace every single test you take.

Yes, books are lovely, dark, and deep,
But only what you grasp you keep,
With hours to go before you sleep,
With hours to go before you sleep.

CONTENTS

CONTEXT

JEANNE WAKATSUKI WAS BORN on September 26, 1934, in Inglewood, California, to George Ko Wakatsuki and Riku Sugai Wakatsuki. She spent her early childhood in Ocean Park, California, where her father was a fisherman. She spent her teenage years in Long Beach, California, and San Jose, California. After a brief period in Long Beach after World War II, her family finally settled in San Jose, where her father took up berry farming. Wakatsuki received a degree in journalism from San Jose State University in 1956 and a year later married her classmate and fellow writer John D. Houston. John Houston's tour in the United States Air Force took them to England, and eventually to France, where Jeanne studied French civilization at the Sorbonne, a prestigious university in Paris. She has been honored with many awards and prizes, including the 1979 Woman of Achievement Award from the National Women's Political Caucus and a 1976 Humanitas Prize for her television adaptation of *Farewell to Manzanar*. Her other works include *Beyond Manzanar: Views of Asian American Womanhood*; *Don't Cry, It's Only Thunder*, co-authored with Paul Hensler; and numerous essays and articles. *Farewell to Manzanar*, her most famous work, recounts the three years she and her family spent as prisoners at Manzanar Relocation Center in the desert of southeastern California.

Farewell to Manzanar begins with the U.S. entry into World War II after the Japanese attack on Pearl Harbor in 1942, three years after war had begun raging in Europe. Despite Europe's calls for American aid, U.S. public opinion was divided between isolationists, who did not see the German dictator Adolf Hitler as a threat to the United States, and the interventionists, who, led by President Franklin D. Roosevelt, saw fascism as a global menace. The compromise reached by these two groups was a policy called Lend-Lease, which allowed the United States to aid the Allied forces with military supplies and food in exchange for military bases in British and French territories in the Caribbean and Pacific. The United States was generally more concerned with protecting itself than with curbing the combined Axis powers of Germany and Italy. When Japan joined the Axis, the United States continued to refrain from intervening and chose to respond with what President Roosevelt called "measures short of war," this time in the form of an embargo on scrap iron and steel shipments to Japan. Japanese military leader General Hideki Tojo sent representatives to Washington, D.C., to negotiate. But on December 7, 1941, while negotiations were in progress, the Japanese attacked the headquarters of the U.S. Navy's Pacific fleet at Pearl Harbor, Hawaii, killing over 2,500 people and severely crippling the U.S. fleet. President Roosevelt called the attack on Pearl Harbor "a date which will live in infamy." Three days later the United States declared war on Japan. The declaration of war made many Americans view Japanese not just as unwanted aliens but as enemies to be feared. This irrational fear was the most direct cause of the internment of people of Japanese descent, which Wakatsuki describes in *Farewell to Manzanar.*

JAPANESE IMMIGRATION & RELOCATION

Jeanne Wakatsuki's father was part of the first group of Japanese people who immigrated to the United States, Hawaii, Latin America, and Europe, who were called *Issei,* which literally means "first generation" in Japanese. Those who immigrated to the United States worked mainly as farmers, fisherman, servants, and other unskilled laborers, but many eventually went to school and became professional workers. A series of laws passed in the early twentieth century tried to stop immigration from Japan by preventing Issei from applying for naturalization and owning land in California. In 1924, the U.S. Congress passed an Immigration Act that ended all Japanese immigration. The children of the Issei were called *Nisei,* which means "second generation" in Japanese. Unlike their Issei parents, the Nisei were Americans by virtue of being born in the United States, and they adopted American language and customs more easily. Wakatsuki was herself among the Nisei, who were educated primarily in the United States, spoke little or no Japanese, and knew very little about Japan.

Although hatred of Asians and Asian Americans has existed in the United States since the first arrival of Chinese miners and railroad workers in the mid-nineteenth century, the attack on Pearl Harbor sparked a new period of overt racial fear. This hysteria culminated in the U.S. War Department's adoption of the Japanese-American relocation program recounted in *Farewell to Manzanar.* Manzanar, the camp in which the Wakatsuki family was imprisoned for three years during the war, opened in 1942 and was the first of ten identical camps scattered throughout the western states. For three years, Manzanar was home to over 11,000 people and consisted of close to 800 buildings. On December 18, 1944, the Supreme Court finally ruled that imprisonment of Nisei constituted the illegal imprisonment of loyal U.S. citizens. But though the high court ordered the camps to be shut down, it still took a full year for all of them to close officially. For years the camps' survivors fought for compensation for the relocation policy, and in 1988 President Ronald Reagan finally signed a bill guaranteeing $20,000 to every living survivor of the camps. In 1990 President George Bush made a public apology to Japanese Americans imprisoned during the war and in 1992 declared Manzanar a National Historic Site.

PLOT OVERVIEW

IN THE MORNING OF DECEMBER 7, 1941, Jeanne Wakatsuki says farewell to Papa's sardine fleet at San Pedro Harbor in California. But soon the boats return, and news reaches the family that the Japanese have bombed Pearl Harbor in Hawaii. Papa burns his Japanese flag and identity papers but is arrested by the FBI. Mama moves the family to the Japanese ghetto on Terminal Island and then to Boyle Heights in Los Angeles. President Roosevelt's Executive Order 9066, which he signs in February 1942, gives the military the authority to relocate potential threats to national security. Those of Japanese descent in America can only await their final destination: "their common sentiment is *shikata ga nai*" ("it cannot be helped"). One month later, the government orders the Wakatsukis to move to Manzanar Relocation Center in the desert 225 miles northeast of Los Angeles.

Upon arriving in the camp, the Japanese Americans find cramped living conditions, badly prepared food, unfinished barracks, and swirling dust that blows in through every crack and knothole. There is not enough warm clothing to go around, many people fall ill from immunizations and poorly preserved food, and they must face the indignity of the nonpartitioned camp toilets, an insult that particularly affects Mama. The Wakatsukis stop eating together in the camp mess halls, and the family begins to disintegrate. Jeanne, virtually abandoned by her family, takes an interest in the other people in camp and begins studying religious questions with a pair of nuns. However, after Jeanne experiences sunstroke while imagining herself as a suffering saint, Papa orders her to stop.

Papa is arrested and returns a year later. He has been at Fort Lincoln detention camp. The family is unsure how to greet him. Only Jeanne welcomes him openly. Jeanne has always admired Papa, who left his samurai, or warrior class, family in Japan to protest the declining social status of the samurai. She looks back fondly on the style with which he has always conducted himself, from his courting of Mama to his virtuoso pig carving. Something has happened to Papa, however, during his time at the detention camp, where the government interrogators have accused him of disloyalty and spying. The accusation is an insult and has sent Papa into a downward emotional spiral. He becomes violent and drinks heavily, and nearly strikes Mama with his cane before Kiyo, Papa's youngest son, saves her by punching Papa in the face.

The frustration of the other men in camp eventually results in an event called the December Riot, which breaks out after three men are arrested for beating a man suspected of helping the U.S. government. The rioters roam the camp searching for *inu,* a word that means both "dog" and "traitor" in Japanese. The military police try to put an end to the riot, but in the chaos they shoot into the crowd, killing two Japanese and wounding ten others. The same night, a patrol group accosts Jeanne's brother-in-law Kaz and his fellow workers and accuses them of sabotage. The mess hall bells ring until noon the following day as a memorial to the dead. Soon after, the government issues a Loyalty Oath to distinguish loyal Japanese from potential enemies. Camp opinion about whether to take the oath is divided. Answering "No No" to the loyalty questions will result in deportation, but answering "Yes Yes" will result in being drafted. Both Papa and Woody, one of his sons, endorse the "Yes Yes" position, and Papa attacks a man for calling him an *inu,* or collaborator. That night, Jeanne overhears Papa singing the Japanese national anthem, *Kimi ga yo,* which speaks of the endurance of stones.

After the riots, camp life calms down and the Wakatsuki family moves to a nicer barracks near a pear orchard, where Papa takes up gardening. Manzanar itself begins to resemble a typical American town. Schools open, the residents are allowed to take short trips outside the camp, and Jeanne's oldest brother, Bill, even forms a dance band called The Jive Bombers. Jeanne explores the world inside the camp and tries out various Japanese and American hobbies before taking up baton twirling. She also returns to her religious studies and is just about to be baptized when Papa intervenes. Jeanne begins to distance herself from Papa, while the birth of a grandchild draws Mama and Papa closer than ever.

By the end of 1944, the number of people at Manzanar dwindles as men are drafted and families take advantage of the government's new policy of relocating families away from the west coast. Woody is drafted and, despite Papa's protests, leaves in November to join the famous all-Nisei 442nd Combat Regiment. While in the military, Woody visits Papa's family in Hiroshima, Japan. He meets Toyo, Papa's aunt, and finally understands the origin of Papa's pride. In December, the U.S. Supreme Court rules that the internment policy is illegal, and the War Department begins preparations to close the camps. The remaining residents, out of fear and lack of prospects, try to postpone their departure, but eventually they are ordered to leave. Papa decides to leave in style and buys a broken-down blue sedan to ferry his family back to Long Beach.

In Long Beach, the Wakatsukis move into a housing project called Cabrillo Homes. Though they fear public hatred, they see little sign of it. On the first day of sixth grade, however, a girl in Jeanne's class is amazed at Jeanne's ability to speak English, which makes Jeanne realize that prejudice is not always open and direct. She later becomes close friends with the girl, Radine, who lives in the same housing project. The two share the same activities and tastes, but when they move to high school, unspoken prejudice keeps Jeanne from the social and extracurricular successes available to Radine.

Jeanne retreats into herself and nearly drops out of school, but when Papa moves the family to San Jose to take up berry farming, she decides to make another attempt at school life. Her homeroom nominates her to be queen of the school's annual spring carnival, and for the election assembly she leaves her hair loose and wears an exotic sarong. The teachers try to prevent her from winning, but her friend Leonard Rodriguez uncovers the teachers' plot and ensures her victory. Papa is furious that Jeanne has won the election by flaunting her sexuality in front of American boys. He forces her to take Japanese dance lessons, but she stops taking them after a short time. As a compromise, she wears a conservative dress to the coronation ceremony, but the crowd's muttering makes her realize that neither the exotic sarong nor the conservative dress represents her true self.

In April 1972, much later in life, Jeanne visits the Manzanar site with her husband and two children. She needs to remind herself that the camp actually existed, because over the years she has begun to think she imagined the whole thing. Walking through the ruins, the sounds and images of the camp come back to her. Seeing her eleven-year-old daughter, Jeanne realizes that her life began at the camp just as her father's life ended there. She recalls Papa driving crazily through camp before leaving with his family, and she finally understands his stubborn pride.

Character List

Jeanne Wakatsuki The protagonist and author of *Farewell to Manzanar*. Jeanne is the youngest of the Wakatsuki children and Papa's favorite. She observes and comments on her own and her family's experiences before, during, and after the wartime internment. In the beginning of the narrative she is a naïve seven-year-old, but as she grows older, she loses her naïveté and comes to understand the true nature of the camps, her family, and herself.

Papa (George Ko Wakatsuki) Jeanne's father and the patriarch of the American branch of the Wakatsuki family. Papa is a first-generation Japanese immigrant with a strong sense of honor. His experience shows how unfair accusations hurt many Japanese families: when the FBI accuses Papa of being a Japanese spy, his relationship with his family deteriorates and he becomes an alcoholic.

Mama (Rigu Sukai Wakatsuki) Jeanne's mother. Patient and caring with her children and husband, Mama places a high value on privacy and dignity. Despite Papa's violent treatment of her while at Manzanar, she is the first member of the Wakatsuki family to make amends with Papa, demonstrating her commitment to family.

Woodrow "Woody" Wakatsuki The third Wakatsuki child. Woody is the most fatherly of Jeanne's brothers and takes charge when Papa is detained for a year at Fort Lincoln. Woody demonstrates his loyalty to America by joining the U.S. army.

Kiyo Wakatsuki The ninth Wakatsuki child and Jeanne's closest brother. Kiyo shares many experiences with Jeanne, including being ambushed by children in the Japanese ghetto on Terminal Island and being spat at and called a "dirty Jap" by an old woman in Long Beach.

Eleanor Wakatsuki   The second Wakatsuki child and Jeanne's oldest sister. Eleanor leaves the camp with her husband, Shig, to relocate to Reno, Nevada, but returns to the camp when Shig is drafted. She gives birth to a baby boy, which leads Mama and Papa to a reconciliation.

Bill Wakatsuki   The oldest Wakatsuki child. Along with Woody, Bill serves as one of Papa's crew before the war on his sardine boats. In the camp, he is the leader of a dance band called The Jive Bombers.

Kaz   Jeanne's brother-in-law and Martha's husband. Kaz is stopped by a detachment of frightened military police while monitoring the reservoir with his crew on the night of the December Riot.

Aunt Toyo   Papa's aging aunt in Hiroshima, Japan. Woody visits Toyo in 1946 and is impressed by the dignity of her graceful manner and the rich meal she prepares for him in spite of her family's poverty. Woody comes to see this dignity in the face of difficulty as a Wakatsuki family trait.

Radine   Jeanne's white best friend at Cabrillo Homes in Long Beach after the war. Radine's surprise at Jeanne's ability to speak English makes Jeanne realize that while she will not be attacked for being Japanese, she will always be seen as different and not American. Radine's popularity and recognition in high school further underscore the fundamental difference between her and Jeanne, whose Japanese ancestry makes her an outsider.

Leonard Rodriguez   Jeanne's classmate at her new high school in San Jose. Leonard's willingness to be friends with Jeanne despite her outsider status is admirable and contrasts with their teachers' inherent prejudice against Japanese people.

Interrogator The American military man who questions Papa at Fort Lincoln, North Dakota. The interrogator's grilling of Papa on his personal history and his accusation that Papa supplied oil to Japanese submarines represents the U.S. government's tendency to stereotype Japanese Americans as traitors.

Fred Tayama A leader of the Japanese American Citizens League and suspected collaborator with the U.S. government. On December 5, 1942, Tayama is severely beaten, and the arrest of his attackers leads to the December Riot at Manzanar.

Mitsue Endo, Fred Korematsu, Gordon Hirabayashi The Japanese Americans whose Supreme Court cases lead to the eventual closing of the camps in 1944 and 1945.

Granny Mama's mother, sixty-five at the time of the relocation to Manzanar. Granny's inability to go to the mess halls is one reason that the Wakatsuki family stops eating together.

Chizu Woody's wife. Chizu is on the wharf with Jeanne and Mama when the news of the attack on Pearl Harbor is announced.

ANALYSIS OF MAJOR CHARACTERS

JEANNE

As the narrator of *Farewell to Manzanar,* Jeanne describes events in a very unemotional and observational way, as if looking on from a distance. This tone is effective because it helps her keep the factual accounts of the events she witnesses separate from her emotions at the time she witnesses them. She is careful about how she mixes her own analysis and reflection as a writer with the events she is telling as a narrator. The story tends to come in waves of information, and between waves Jeanne takes a step back and tells us what she thought of things as they were happening and how she thinks of them now. These moments of reflection combined with the way Jeanne freely jumps in time within chapters give the impression that she is writing and commenting on things at the same time that she is remembering them. This narrative style fits with the nature of the work, which focuses in part on coming to terms with one's memories.

Jeanne's observational tone derives partly from her age at the time of the internment. Throughout the memoir she emphasizes that she was young at the time and did not really understand the war or the real motives behind the camp. As a young girl she is unaware that U.S. fear of Japanese people is behind her family's imprisonment. In fact, she does not see the camp as imprisonment at all, but rather as an adventure. As the story goes on and Jeanne gets older, however, her view of the world shifts drastically. The violent change in her father during the internment years and her later discovery of the unspoken prejudice of the world to which she returns reveals to her that the world is more complicated than she originally realized. *Farewell to Manzanar* is a coming-of-age story, and Wakatsuki begins by describing events simply and innocently, much as a child would see them. The discoveries she makes about herself during and after her time at Manzanar give the memoir its structure and allow us to chart Wakatsuki's progress from girl to teenager to woman. The work is a way for Wakatsuki to come to terms with herself, and we must understand how unaware of her ethnicity she was as a child in order to appreciate the maturity she shows later in struggling with prejudice.

Jeanne's experiences with prejudice in her school life after the war constitute the main content of her memoir and develop some of the work's most important themes, such as the danger of racial stereotypes and the difficulty of self-discovery. These two themes converge in her story, for she can discover her true self only by overcoming prejudice and setting aside her own preconceptions about what it means to be either Japanese or American. Only at the carnival queen coronation ceremony at her high school in San Jose does she begin to understand that until she stops pretending to be what she is not, she will never be able to understand who she is.

PAPA

Papa, one of the most complex characters in *Farewell to Manzanar,* is the only character besides Jeanne whose development we see from beginning to end. Wakatsuki uses the character of Papa to explore one of the principal themes of her work: the danger of judging an individual by ethnicity alone. Jeanne's own story addresses this theme as well, but Papa's experiences give us a different and more tragic view of its significance. Jeanne is Japanese by heritage but American by birth, so she really belongs to both Japan and America. Papa, on the other hand, chose to leave his homeland to become a noncitizen in the United States, so in a sense, he belongs nowhere. He has virtually ceased to exist in Japan, where his family buried his memory nine years after his departure. On the other hand, as a noncitizen in the United States he is one of the lowest people in the social order. The only things he has to hold on to are his family, business, house, and pride in having made something of himself in the United States despite the odds stacked against him. His imprisonment, together with the charge of disloyalty leveled at him at Fort Lincoln, strips him of his possessions, tears his family apart, and worst of all, turns his pride into bitterness and anger. He is a tragic figure, and one of the reasons that Wakatsuki rarely places blame in her memoir is that she prefers to discuss the injustice of the internment by showing the extent to which it destroyed the loving man that was once her father.

WOODY

CHARACTER ANALYSIS

Woody is a foil to Papa: his attitudes and personal qualities contrast with and thereby accentuate Papa's. Woody, for example, is always sure of his identity as an American and his responsibility to his family, unlike Papa, who has a complicated identity and who does not always act in the best interest of his family. Wakatsuki uses the frequent arguments between Woody and Papa to highlight the differences between the two men. Their discussion about the idea of Woody fighting in the war on the U.S. side exemplifies these differences. While Papa believes that fighting for the United States would mean fighting for a country that imprisoned him, Woody believes that it is his duty as a U.S. citizen to fight for his country. Having citizenship allows Woody access to jobs, licenses, and other opportunities that are closed to Papa, and he feels that service to his country is the price he must pay for the freedom he enjoys. Papa's experiences during and after the war, on the other hand, disillusion him about his place in America.

THEMES, MOTIFS & SYMBOLS

THEMES

Themes are the fundamental and often universal ideas explored in a literary work.

THE DESTRUCTION OF FAMILY LIFE UNDER INTERNMENT

The Wakatsuki family begins to break down because of how Manzanar forces them to live, but the final blow to the family is the realization that they can no longer depend on Papa's solid character for strength. Wakatsuki traces the beginnings of her family's disintegration to the mess hall lifestyle and the way in which it disrupted the cherished Wakatsuki mealtime ritual. When they stop eating together, the Wakatsukis stop connecting with each other, preferring to spend their daytime hours working or volunteering rather than cooped up together in the cramped barracks. This separation leaves Jeanne free to explore, but it also leaves her without a guide or mentor. She spends much of her time in camp floating from one activity to the next. Papa's return from his arrest as a suspected spy accelerates the erosion of the Wakatsuki family structure. His experiences at Fort Lincoln and the accusation of disloyalty leave him a bitter and disillusioned man. He is no longer the source of strength he was before the war, and his return kills all hope that the family will rally around him as patriarch. That most of the older children eventually abandon Mama and Papa in California and relocate to New Jersey shows the deep divide that Manzanar creates in the once happy Wakatsuki family.

Wakatsuki blames her family's disintegration on the camps rather than on the war because the war has little to do with the overall experience of Manzanar. The outbreak of war leads directly to the creation of camps such as Manzanar, but the war itself belongs to the realm of international politics and is far removed from the daily reality of the Wakatsukis' existence. By frequently pointing out indignities such as the nonpartitioned toilets, Wakatsuki shows how even the smallest elements of camp life contribute to the changes in her family. The inconvenience of the lack of privacy and the overcrowding, among other things, create a physical discomfort that eventually turns into an emotional discomfort. The frustrations of camp life shorten tempers and result in outbursts of violence such as the December Riot and Papa's attempt to beat Mama with his cane. These disturbing images show that the divisions that developed within families and within the Japanese-American community as a whole resulted more from the conditions of life than from the war in general.

THE EVERYDAY NATURE OF PREJUDICE

Wakatsuki avoids portraying open ethnic conflict in her memoir in order to examine more carefully the subtle and often unspoken prejudices that infect everyday life, which are often the most dangerous. There are, of course, rumors of Japanese Americans being beaten and abused after they leave Manzanar, but for the most part the direct, open hatred for which the camp residents have prepared themselves never materializes. This imagined hatred shows the rarity of open hatred compared to deep-seated prejudice. In fact, by imagining that all of white America will hate them, these Japanese Americans are themselves subscribing to a kind of prejudice, forgetting that not all Americans are prowar and anti-Japanese. Many Americans, such as Jeanne's kind schoolteachers and the American Friends Service that helps them find housing, actually help the Japanese. The mistaken belief that white America has an all-encompassing hatred for them handicaps the Japanese Americans. They focus so much on what seems to them an inevitable clash that they are not prepared for the subtler prejudice of daily life that is racism's most common face.

The unfortunate result of this everyday nature of prejudice is that the prejudice becomes so ingrained that one can begin to forget that it is in fact a prejudice. Radine's innocent surprise at Jeanne's ability to speak English, for example, makes Jeanne realize that prejudice is not always a conscious choice but that it can also be a result of conditioning by one's parents and culture. Radine judges from Jeanne's Japanese appearance that she shouldn't be able to speak English, because Radine's family or culture (or both) has taught her to do so. Similarly, Jeanne begins to see the entire relocation of Japanese Americans as a function of the government's inability to see good behind a Japanese face. She is shocked to discover that people do not really look to see who she is as a person but instead instantly judge her as a foreigner and paint her with the traits they imagine all Japanese people have. Racial stereotyping was a major part of the U.S. government's wartime propaganda campaign, and many people based their views of Japanese people on the government's attempt to portray them as vicious and subhuman. This propaganda was very effective, and at the height of the war, the derogatory word "Jap" was widely accepted.

THE DIFFICULTY OF UNDERSTANDING ONE'S IDENTITY

The isolated location of Manzanar and the disintegration of the Wakatsuki family during the internment years give young Jeanne a lot of personal space in which to develop an understanding of who she is. The climax of her self-understanding comes much later in life with her return to Manzanar as an adult, which enables her to understand just how much the camp changed her. But with her independence at Manzanar, the young Jeanne begins to learn about the important components of her identity. Papa occasionally tries to correct what he sees as unacceptable behavior, such as smiling too much or studying religion, but ultimately Jeanne does what she wants. Her explorations of Japanese and American activities are early, unconscious attempts to define herself. Since she finds herself surrounded by only Japanese for the first time in her life, she naturally begins to feel the conflict of being both Japanese and American.

Although Manzanar makes Jeanne look more closely at her fellow Japanese, she is unable to resolve the confusion she feels as a Japanese American because the camp isolates her from the American half of her identity. After she leaves Manzanar, the shock of ethnic prejudice compels her to try to reclaim her American identity by fitting in, but her continual attempts to conform to white America's definition of social achievement lead her to neglect the Japanese side of herself. The distance she puts between herself and her Japanese ancestry mirrors the unhealthy isolation from American culture that she experiences at Manzanar. The naïve belief that she can escape her Japanese face and make the world see her as only American leads to her downfall, for when she realizes that people will never see her as truly American, she is left with nothing. Only after changing high schools and being elected carnival queen does she finally see the absurdity of her attempts to define herself as either Japanese or American. Neither an exotic sarong nor an all-American prom dress can completely define her, just as she cannot say she is only Japanese or only American. In searching to define herself according to what others expect, she has ignored who she really is: a Japanese American.

MOTIFS

Motifs are recurring structures, contrasts, or literary devices that can help to develop and inform the text's major themes.

DISPLACEMENT

The Wakatsuki family's frequent moves emphasize the difficulty they and other Japanese have in settling down permanently and reflect their deeper struggle to connect themselves to either Japanese or American culture. The Wakatsukis are comfortably settled in their Ocean Park home, but when they must leave this home behind, they become disoriented and lost, and remain so for the rest of the memoir. In a series of forced and often sudden moves, the Wakatsukis must pack up or sell their belongings and set out for ghettos—Terminal Island, Boyle Heights, and Cabrillo Homes—or for the relocation camp at Manzanar. The overall sense is that the Japanese are being shifted between temporary situations, all the while reaching out for a place to establish a permanent foothold. Ironically, Manzanar, originally a prison to the Japanese, becomes this foothold, and the Japanese are reluctant to let it go after the war. The dark undertone to the motif of displacement is that even if the Japanese do establish more permanent roots somewhere, another war or outbreak of prejudice against them could uproot them just as quickly as before.

AMERICANA

The Japanese Americans at Manzanar latch onto typical elements of American culture in order to show that they are not foreigners or enemies but rather loyal citizens whose only world is America. Even the Issei immigrants had made a conscious choice to come to the United States, and many, like Papa, adopt American ways of life in order to make up for what they lack in legal citizenship. The residents at Manzanar recreate many of the aspects of American life that they like most, such as glee clubs, block associations, high school yearbooks, touch football teams, and even dance bands. For those born in America or long since departed from Japan, America is their only reference point, and they hold on to American culture as something they can share without fueling the anti-Japanese suspicions of government officials. Ironically, the all-Japanese Manzanar is where the Japanese can enjoy the simple pleasures of American culture. The ethnic prejudice of the society outside Manzanar spoils the Japanese people's enjoyment of American culture, as when Jeanne's high school teachers plot to prevent her from winning the carnival queen election.

SYMBOLS

Symbols are objects, characters, figures, or colors used to represent abstract ideas or concepts.

STONES

Stones appear throughout *Farewell to Manzanar* as symbols of Japanese endurance. The Japanese national anthem, *Kimi ga yo,* which Papa sings after getting in a fight, establishes the image of stones that remain unchanged throughout the ages as well as the layers of thick moss that make the stones look bigger than they are. This image suggests that the Japanese ability to endure the trials of Manzanar could actually lead to growth. It is not easy for Jeanne to bear ethnic prejudice, but her endurance enables her to see past the prejudice and discover her identity. Stones also represent solace and rest. For example, the Issei men gather small stones to create tranquil rock gardens, and Papa gazes at the massive Sierra Nevada mountains to escape his thoughts. These rocks remain even when Jeanne returns to the camp nearly thirty years later. The endurance of the rock gardens and the concrete foundations suggest that the camp will continue to exist through the experiences of those who inhabited it.

JEANNE'S DREAM

The blonde prom queen of Jeanne's dream symbolizes Jeanne's American standards of beauty as a young girl as well as her desire to be accepted and admired by her peers. However, the window through which Jeanne watches the girl symbolizes the barrier of ethnic prejudice that lets her see her goal but never achieve it. As Jeanne fights against more and more prejudice over time, this dream comes to symbolize the hopelessness she feels at being excluded from the social world open to her white friend Radine. That the dream persists even after her prom queen dreams are long behind her suggests that Jeanne has not entirely found what she is looking for and that ethnic prejudice still stands in the way of what she wants to achieve in life.

SUMMARY & ANALYSIS

CHAPTER I

SUMMARY—"WHAT IS PEARL HARBOR?"

On Sunday, December 7, 1941, seven-year-old Jeanne Wakatsuki watches from the Long Beach, California, wharf as a fleet of sardine boats prepares to leave the harbor. Her father, whom she calls "Papa," yells more than the other men. He barks orders at his two eldest sons, Bill and Woody, who act as his crew. Papa is aboard the larger of his two boats, the *Nereid*, which he pays for by giving percentages of his catch to the large canneries on Terminal Island, near Long Beach. Many other fishermen have similar arrangements with the canneries, and they often fish together. Jeanne and her family stand on the wharf and wave goodbye until the boats have nearly disappeared. Suddenly the fleet stops and floats on the horizon like white gulls. Jeanne's mother, whom she calls "Mama," and Woody's wife, Chizu, begin to worry when the fleet turns back toward the port. The other women wonder whether there has been an accident. When the boats are still a half mile offshore, a cannery worker runs along the docks reporting that Japan has bombed Pearl Harbor. Chizu asks Mama what Pearl Harbor is. Mama does not know and shouts after the man, but he is already gone.

That night Papa burns the Japanese flag he brought with him from Hiroshima thirty-five years earlier. He also burns any documents that might connect him with Japan. He is worried because he is a non-U.S. citizen with a fishing license, and the FBI has begun arresting such people as potential spies. The family goes to stay on Terminal Island with Woody, but two weeks later, two FBI men arrest Papa. Jeanne thinks the FBI men look like characters from a 1930s movie. Papa does not resist arrest, but walks out tall and dignified ahead of the two men. The FBI interrogates many Japanese and begins searching Terminal Island for material that could be used for spying, such as short-wave radio antennae, flashlights, cameras, and even toy swords. The family learns that Papa has been taken into custody, but the sons are unable to find out where he has been taken. An article in the next day's paper reports that Papa has been arrested for supplying oil to a Japanese submarine. Mama cries for

days, but Jeanne does not cry at all. She does not fully understand
Mama's grief until she finally sees Papa again a year later.

─────────────

ANALYSIS

Wakatsuki begins her memoir with an idyllic portrait of prewar
American life in order to foreshadow the suddenness of the attack
on Pearl Harbor and the United States' entry into World War II. In
1941, the war had been raging in Europe for over two years, but the
United States had remained neutral, and Wakatsuki's writing
reflects the carefree point of view of the youngest child of a middle-
class American family far removed from concerns of politics and
war. Her father, who has just purchased his own fishing boat, is living the American dream: he has his own business, grown sons to
help him, and a family of ten children who come down to the docks
to see him off. Wakatsuki's many references to the warm December
weather, her father's cooperative colleagues, and an ideal environment where the water is clean and the California air is smog-free
leave us as unprepared for war as Jeanne and her family are at the
beginning of the memoir. In Jeanne's eyes, all is well with the world,
and nothing seems to threaten her family's harmonious existence.

In one of *Farewell to Manzanar*'s most dramatic passages,
Wakatsuki recounts the news of the Pearl Harbor attack not
through direct narration but through an image. The striking picture
of the entire fleet of departing boats stopping suddenly and silently
on the horizon creates an immediate sense that something has gone
wrong. With her description of the slow, silent return of the boats
and the worried questions of the family members, Wakatsuki creates a dramatic tension that is released, at least partially, when the
cannery worker relays the news of the attack. This kind of tension is
called *dramatic irony,* a literary technique in which the audience
knows something that the characters do not. Wakatsuki combines
our knowledge of the events at Pearl Harbor with the fact that Mama
and Chizu do not even know what Pearl Harbor is to underscore the
Japanese Americans' innocence and sense of bewilderment upon hearing of Japan's attack on what they consider to be their home. The
naïveté of this bewilderment is touching, and it is sad that a place they
have never heard of will soon be the cause of their unhappiness.

Wakatsuki establishes Papa as a dynamic and ultimately likeable
character early on in order to show us how greatly the anti-Japanese
prejudice in the United States destroys him. The picture she paints of
Papa as a tall and brash "skipper" with rough manners and an inde-

pendent spirit shows Papa in a very American light. His struggle to reconcile these adopted customs and characteristics with his true Japanese ancestry becomes one of the main threads of Wakatsuki's story. She sets up this struggle in the first chapter by establishing Papa as both the most American and the most Japanese of all the characters. He is an alien without citizenship, but he seems to believe firmly in the American dream, and after learning of the Pearl Harbor attack, he even goes so far as to burn his Japanese flag and documents in order to distance himself from Japan. The tragedy of Papa's story is that his sacrifice is for nothing: the very United States that he calls home and for which he has forsaken his homeland accuses him of spying and betrayal. The last image of him in this chapter is of a dignified prisoner striding confidently ahead of his accusers, enduring his fate with the same quiet patience with which his family and people endure theirs. It is his last moment of real dignity in the memoir and marks the beginning of bad times for both the Wakatsuki family and the Japanese Americans in general.

CHAPTER 2

SUMMARY — SHIKATA GA NAI

Soon after Papa's arrest, Mama relocates the family to the Japanese immigrant ghetto on Terminal Island. Mama feels more comfortable in the company of other Japanese, but the new environment of Terminal Island frightens Jeanne. It is the first time she has lived among other Japanese, and she traces her fear to an earlier time, when Papa threatened to sell her to the "Chinaman" if she behaved badly. Mama and Chizu go to work for the canneries that own the island, and the family takes up residence in a barracks alongside the other migrant workers. Jeanne feels uncomfortable around the rough youth who proudly call themselves *yogore* ("uncouth ones") and pick on outsiders and people who do not speak their language. The other second-graders tease Jeanne for not speaking Japanese, and both she and her ten-year-old brother, Kiyo, must avoid the children's ambushes after school.

The family lives on Terminal Island for two months, and on February 25, 1942 the government decides to move the Japanese farther away from the Long Beach Naval Station. The family, including Granny, Jeanne's sixty-five-year-old maternal grandmother, is given forty-eight hours to leave. Mama has to sell her china because it will not fit in Woody's car. When a secondhand dealer insults her by offering only fifteen dollars for the china, she angrily smashes the entire set in front of him.

The family settles in the minority ghetto of Boyle Heights in downtown Los Angeles. President Roosevelt has signed Executive Order 9066, which authorizes the War Department to remove persons considered threats to national security from military areas on the West Coast, and rumors begin to circulate about relocation. Mama finally receives a letter from Papa, who is being held at Fort Lincoln, a camp for enemy aliens in North Dakota. The Japanese both comfort themselves and excuse the U.S. government's actions with the phrase "*shikata ga nai*," which means both "it cannot be helped" and "it must be done." Kiyo and Jeanne enroll in school, but Jeanne does not like the cold, distant teacher, who is the first Caucasian from whom she has felt hostility.

The public attitude toward the Japanese soon turns to fear, and a month after the Wakatsuki family settles in Boyle Heights, the government orders the Japanese to move again, this time to the relocation camp at Manzanar, California. Many Japanese accept the move because they are afraid of Caucasian aggression, but some simply see it as an adventure. A bus picks up the Wakatsukis at a Buddhist temple, and each family receives an identification number and tags to put on their collars. Jeanne falls asleep on the bus, nearly half of which is filled with her relatives, and wakes up to the setting sun and the yellow, billowing dust of Owens Valley. As they enter the camp, the new arrivals stare silently at the families already waiting in the wind and sand.

The bus arrives in time for dinner, but the Japanese are horrified to learn that the cooks have poured canned apricots over the rice, a staple the Japanese do not eat with sweet foods. After dinner, the Wakatsukis are taken to a wooden barracks in Block 16, where they receive two sixteen-by-twenty-foot rooms for the twelve members of the family. They divide the space with blankets and sleep on mattress covers stuffed with straw. The younger couples have a hard time adjusting to the lack of privacy, and six months later Jeanne's sister and her husband leave to help harvest beets in Idaho. Jeanne does not mind the tight quarters, because it means she gets to sleep with Mama.

Analysis

Jeanne's instant sense of alienation among other Japanese creates an initial picture of her as more American than Japanese. As a Nisei, or second-generation Japanese American born to immigrant parents,

Jeanne is a U.S. citizen by birth. She has grown up in a Caucasian neighborhood, and she feels awkward now when plunged into the immigrant community of Terminal Island. Her description of the rough and tumble immigrant community as "a country as foreign as India or Arabia would have been" shows her inability to relate to other native Japanese. Her western name and fear of Asian faces do not help her fit in, but her greatest obstacle is her inability to speak Japanese, which the tough Terminal Island kids insist on speaking. Her comment that the Japanese children despised her for speaking English establishes the theme of ethnic prejudice that runs throughout the memoir. This harsh treatment at the hands of her own people contrasts with the pleasantness of her earlier life—her family's big, American-style frame house in the non-Japanese neighborhood of Ocean Park, for example, and her grandmotherly non-Japanese teacher who cried the day Jeanne had to leave. This kind America is all Jeanne has ever known, and she presents herself here not as a Japanese thrown into solidarity with her people but as an American forced to live among an alien race.

The U.S. government's increased manipulation of the Japanese people strengthens the Japanese community. This sense of community is largely a response to the tension that develops between Japanese and Americans as American soldiers impose their will upon the Japanese. The contrast between the family's initial move to Terminal Island, which Mama initiates, and their relocation to Boyle Heights, which the United States government requires, shows how fighting against oppression unites the Japanese. Upon arriving at Terminal Island, the family does not immediately befriend the other Japanese people. However, when the government orders a relocation, the Japanese band together in their fear and uncertainty as they wait for the inevitable order to move from Terminal Island. Wakatsuki describes a communal sentiment with the Japanese phrase "*shikata ga nai,*" the sense that there is nothing one can do. Even Jeanne, who thinks of herself as American and of the Japanese as an alien people, experiences this feeling of resignation when her new white teacher treats her coldly. In a critical time, Jeanne, like other Japanese Americans, finds her people a source of comfort.

Wakatsuki sees pride as a defining characteristic of the Japanese people and explores it as both a liability and a strength. The rough Japanese kids of Terminal Island are proud of their derogatory nickname, "*yogore,*" and of their ethnicity and culture, even to the point of excluding one of their own who does not speak their language.

While Wakatsuki initially casts this pride in a negative light, she also shows how it can become a powerful tool when the Japanese are faced with prejudice and the prospect of relocation. Jeanne's mother's decision to smash her china rather that sell it to the scheming secondhand dealer demonstrates that money is not as important to her as her integrity. Similarly, the Japanese people's refusal to eat apricots with their rice is their small, dignified way of signaling to the American government that while they cannot resist forced relocation, they will not accept a slap in the face. These small, pride-won victories keep the Japanese grounded in their culture, which helps keep them unified as a people.

CHAPTERS 3–4

SUMMARY — CHAPTER 3: A DIFFERENT KIND OF SAND

The Wakatsukis wake up early the first morning in Manzanar covered in gray dust that has blown through the knotholes in the walls and floor. They have used their clothes as bedding for extra warmth, and nearly everything they own has been soiled. Jeanne and Kiyo find their predicament funny, but Mama does not. Woody calls through the wall, jokingly asking if they have fallen into the same flour barrel as him. Kiyo replies that they have not, joking that theirs is "full of Japs." The children dress quickly, and Woody instructs Jeanne's brothers Ray and Kiyo to cover the knotholes with tin can lids while Jeanne and her sister May sweep the floor and fold laundry. Woody threatens to make the boys eat any sand that comes up through the knotholes. When Kiyo asks about the sand that comes in through the cracks, Woody jokes that it is a different kind of sand and, mimicking Papa's voice, says he knows the difference. The wind continues to blow dust through the floor. Mama asks Woody to cover the cracks. He promises to patch the cracks with scrap lumber, but she is not satisfied, decrying the horrid conditions. Woody promises to make the repair job better and goes out to see what is for breakfast. Kiyo jokes that it will be hotcakes with soy sauce, but Woody says it will be rice with maple syrup and butter.

SUMMARY — CHAPTER 4: A COMMON MASTER PLAN

> *Mama knew cooperation was the only way to survive.*
> *At the same time she placed a high premium on personal*
> *privacy. Almost everyone at Manzanar had inherited*
> *this pair of traits from the generations before them.*
>
> *(See* QUOTATIONS, *p. 61)*

The Wakatsukis wait in the cold for half an hour for breakfast and eat huddled around the oil stove that Woody has repaired. He begins fixing things, but it is months before the family's quality of life improves. Wakatsuki tells us that the Japanese were not ready for the camps, and the camps were not ready for the Japanese. She says that the Japanese, not knowing what to expect, did not bring enough warm clothing for the April weather and high altitude. The War Department begins issuing World War I surplus clothing, most of which is too large for the Japanese. A makeshift clothing factory is soon set up, and dozens of seamstresses convert the surplus into more practical articles of clothing.

Almost nothing works in the camps, and the children are continually sick due to typhoid immunizations and food spoiled by inexperienced cooks and poor refrigeration. Bowel problems known as the "Manzanar runs" become part of daily life for young and old alike. On the first morning, Jeanne and Mama try to use the latrine in their block but discover that the toilets are overflowing onto the already excrement-covered floor. They try another latrine two blocks away. The latrine is like every other latrine in each of the ten camps, which were all built according to the same plan. The toilets are back to back, with no partitions. One old woman sets up a cardboard box around her toilet as a makeshift partition. She offers the partition to Mama, who graciously accepts it. Cardboard partitions become widely used until wooden partitions arrive, but many people choose to wait to use the bathroom until late at night for more privacy. Like many Japanese, Mama never gets used to the latrines because she places a high value on privacy, but she endures them because she knows that cooperation is the only way to survive.

ANALYSIS — CHAPTER 3

Although *Farewell to Manzanar* is part of the genre of childhood memoirs of war and war camp life, which includes *Night,* by Elie Weisel, and Anne Frank's *The Diary of a Young Girl,* it is primarily a bildungsroman, or coming-of-age story, that deals with the transition from childhood innocence to adult knowledge. Wakatsuki begins her memoir from the humorously naïve perspective of her seven-year-old self so that we may see more clearly the changes the camp causes in her over the course of her three years there. Her carefree attitude upon arriving at Manzanar rubs off on her siblings, and their jokes the first morning (about the dust, among other things) reflect their view that the camp is more an adventure than a hardship. the joy that infuses the Wakatsuki children this first morning in the camp barracks is both comforting and disturbing. Ten-year-old Kiyo's assertion that he has fallen into a flour barrel "full of Japs" shows his easygoing nature but also reveals how greatly he fails to realize the gravity of his family's new circumstances. Uninformed for the moment about the war and the biased motives behind the internment, the younger Wakatsuki children view the camp as something of a game. Only when they are mature enough to understand the prejudice against them do their impressions of the camp change.

ANALYSIS — CHAPTER 4

Mama's shock upon arriving at the camp contrasts with the children's strange glee and is closer to the reaction we expect from someone so suddenly uprooted from his or her home. Mama's stunned silence upon first seeing the dust-covered room gives us a glimpse of the real pain the relocation caused the Japanese Americans. Whereas the children joke about the cracks, the knotholes, and the uninsulated clapboard walls, Mama sees them for the terrible living conditions they represent. Mama's perspective slowly reveals to us what camp conditions were actually like: there is little warm clothing or privacy, and people are continually sick from eating spoiled food. Japanese culture places high value on privacy and cleanliness, and the American government insults the Japanese greatly by giving them no way to act according to these values.

Cooperation is crucial to the Japanese attempts to make do in the ill-prepared and ill-managed camp. The camp inhabitants' endurance and solidarity is surprisingly widespread, but it could be that Wakatsuki chooses not to tell us about the anger and frustration boiling under the surface in order to focus on the inhabitants' strength in the face of adversity. They believe that working together to survive, such as by sewing usable garments out of surplus material and sharing cardboard toilet partitions, is more productive than fighting against their oppressors. Wakatsuki views this kind of cooperation as particularly Japanese. The fact that cooperation does not manifest itself as mass resistance or protest can be explained by the common sentiment that the camp's residents express: "*shikata ga nai.*" This expression embodies the combination of resignation and motivation that the Japanese display throughout *Farewell to Manzanar.*

CHAPTER 5

SUMMARY—ALMOST A FAMILY

Jeanne notices that after a few weeks, her family stops eating together in mess halls. She remembers that before entering the camp, her family used to enjoy noisy, homegrown meals around a large, round wooden table. Now, however, Granny is too weak to go to the mess hall, and Jeanne's older siblings often eat with friends in other mess halls where the food is better, while the younger brothers make a game of trying to eat in as many different mess halls as possible in a single meal period. Jeanne and Kiyo often eat with other children, away from the adults. Wakatsuki notes that later in the war, sociologists noticed the division occurring within families, and the camp authorities tried unsuccessfully to force families to eat together. But camp life accelerated the disintegration of the Wakatsuki family—the barracks were too small for Mama to cook in, and there was no privacy. Wakatsuki says that the closing of the camps made this fragmentation worse, since the older children moved away and the remaining family members had to eat in shifts in a tiny apartment. She adds that after being released, she wrote a paper for her journalism class about how her family used to catch and eat fish together at their home in Ocean Park. She closed the paper by saying that she wanted to remember this experience because she knew she would never be able to have it again.

Back in the camp, a call goes out for volunteer workers, and many Japanese sign up. Jeanne's brothers sign up as carpenters, roofers, and reservoir crewmembers, and Mama begins to earn nineteen dollars a month as a dietician helping the camp cooks. She works in order to pay the warehouse in Los Angeles, where she has stored the family furniture. She worries about Papa, from whom she receives occasional letters, but starts to ignore Jeanne. Jeanne looks for attention elsewhere and begins to observe the other people in camp. In hot weather she watches the 10,000 people walking around the camp at night. She pays special attention to a half-black woman who is masquerading as Japanese to stay with her husband; an aristocratic woman who whitens her face with rice flour; a pair of pale, thin-lipped nurses who look like traditional Japanese kabuki theater actors; and Japanese nuns. The nuns run an orphanage in the camp with Father Steinbeck, who is white, and they nearly convert Jeanne to Catholicism before Papa intervenes. Jeanne is attracted to the stories of saints and martyrs, and spends nearly every afternoon and all day Sunday with the sisters. Walking home in the hot sun, she likes to imagine that she too is suffering with the martyrs. One day, however, she suffers sunstroke and does not go back to her religious study for a month.

Just before Jeanne's bout of sunstroke, Papa returns to Manzanar, and the whole family goes out to greet him. Woody's wife, Chizu, is absent because she has just given birth to a son, whom she has named George in honor of Papa's return. When the bus door opens, the first thing Jeanne sees is a cane. Papa is thin, and withered, and he favors his right leg. He and the family look at each other in silence, and only Jeanne has the courage to approach him. She runs to him, hugs his legs, and begins to cry.

———————————————

ANALYSIS

Wakatsuki concentrates her memoir on her family's breakup rather than on the war itself because the disintegration of her family's structure is much closer to her heart. In general, young Jeanne focuses on immediate concerns rather than broad ones. Instead of blaming the war or the government for her family's estrangement, for example, she specifically blames the mess hall lifestyle that the camp forces her family to adopt. Before the war, mealtime, with Papa at its head, was the most important part of her family life, but now Papa is gone and impersonal mess halls have replaced the family's big, wooden dinner table. However, the family members themselves contribute to their own breakup. Her descriptions of how her various siblings eat in various mess halls reveals her pain at her family's lack of effort to stay together in Papa's absence. Ironically, the government itself tries to reestablish family life by requiring families to eat together. Unfortunately, in a camp of 10,000 people, where many family members are missing, forcing families together is as impossible as it is absurd. For Wakatsuki, the true tragedy of Manzanar is not the abstract injustice of imprisoning a people but that it stripped her of something very precious to her—her happy family.

Though the Wakatsuki's are eager to see Papa again, his return proves a foreshadowing of bad things to come. So many hardships have beset the family during Papa's absence that it seems as though his arrival should herald a return to normalcy. His arrival does briefly counteract the disintegration of the family, as most of the family comes out together to welcome him. Even Woody's wife, Chizu, who has just given birth, pays homage to Papa by naming her son after him. The family is united in their excitement, but when the bus door opens, their expectations are dimmed. The first thing they see of Papa is a cane, a sign of lameness and an immediate indication that he has changed for the worse. Wakatsuki describes him as gaunt and "wilted as his shirt," a completely different man from the gruff and strong sailor she describes in "What is Pearl Harbor?" This physical change reflects a deeper change in him, and the fact that only Jeanne runs to meet him demonstrates her continuing naïveté with regard to the war and the internment. She can see him only as the same man she has always known him to be, and only later does she realize the deep changes that his time in Fort Lincoln brought about in him.

Wakatsuki's focus on her family's struggle to cope with their estrangement rather than on the estrangement itself suggests that working through difficulties was a more important part of life at Manzanar than were the difficulties themselves. The narrative structure of "Almost a Family" is unusual in that it glosses over the details of the family's collapse. We might expect Wakatsuki to show us these dramatic moments, but she focuses instead on the family at its lowest point. In the middle of the chapter, for example, the family members are almost all working and seem to have found ways to fill the void left by their damaged family life. Jeanne, specifically, amuses herself by wandering the camp and watching the faces of various strangers. With Papa's return, the family reassembles and tries to reconstruct a version of itself around him. But the Wakatsukis, and we as well, soon realize that this effort is futile. The depressing significance of the chapter's title, "Almost a Family," becomes clear: no matter how much they might try to become a functional family again, the Wakatsukis will never be able to repair the damage the camps have done.

CHAPTER 6

SUMMARY & ANALYSIS

SUMMARY—WHATEVER HE DID HAD FLOURISH

Papa continues to use his cane even after he recovers. Sometimes he uses it as a sword to swat at his family, and Jeanne imagines it as a makeshift version of the samurai sword of his great-great-grandfather from Hiroshima. Jeanne sees the camp as the place where her father's life ends and her own life begins.

Papa is the oldest son of a samurai family that was stripped of its warrior status when Commodore Matthew Perry arrived in Japan. Papa's uncle was a general and persuaded him to enter military school, but he dropped out at seventeen and sailed for the Hawaiian Islands with money borrowed from an aunt. In Hawaii, Papa saw an advertisement for a job. He bought a new suit and went to find out about the job, but on arriving he found that the ad was for work in the sugar cane fields. He soon found a job as a houseboy in Idaho for an American lawyer. After spending five years with the lawyer, he enrolled at the University of Idaho and began preparing for a law degree. He changed his plans, however, when he met Jeanne's mother.

Mama was born in Hawaii to a sugar cane worker from Niigata, Japan. Her family moved to Spokane, Washington, after her birth. When Mama was seventeen, she had already been promised to the son of a well-to-do farmer. She met Papa one morning when he was unloading vegetables at a market. Her family did not like him because he lived a fast-paced life, but the two eloped and got married in Salem, Oregon. They moved frequently over the next eighteen years and had ten children. Papa did not finish law school and worked many odd jobs. A few years before Jeanne was born he started farming near Watsonville, California. During the Great Depression he moved to Inglewood, but he then turned to fishing in Santa Monica, where he acquired two boats, a house, and a Studebaker.

Jeanne sees her parents' golden wedding anniversary as the climax of her family's happiness at Ocean Park. She recalls that her father stood looking elegant in his double-breasted suit and demonstrated how to carve a pig with a few swift strokes of a cleaver. Jeanne says that her father was not a great man but that he held on to his self-respect and dreams, and whatever he did, he did with flourish. She adds that the other men at the detention camp at Fort Lincoln remember him because he helped the government conduct interviews, taught other inmates English, and gave comic readings of the news every morning.

ANALYSIS

Papa is unique in the memoir both because he is an Issei, or first-generation Japanese immigrant, and because of the status that his family's samurai heritage confers upon him. The U.S. government's disregard for the historical importance of the samurai class reflects the extent to which its actions degrade Papa. For centuries Japan was a feudal society ruled by samurai warlords, but when Commodore Perry forced Japan to open its ports to the West in 1853, the feudal structure crumbled. However, the social significance of having samurai heritage remained powerful. But Papa's high social status in Japan contrasts sharply with the working class status he must assume in America, where he does not own land or automatically earn respect from others. Rather, he must move frequently in order to catch odd jobs, repeatedly starting his life from scratch.

Papa's identification with his samurai heritage explains the high value he places on honor and his concern about being disgraced. The samurai were long important and greatly respected members of Japanese society. Papa feels shame about his father's cabaret business, because the working-class nature of such an enterprise has reduced his father from a noble individual to an average worker. The extent of Papa's shame is manifest in his cutting himself off from his family; he does not want his father's disgrace to taint him. His abandonment of his family constitutes a figurative version of the suicide that disgraced samurai are expected to commit. Papa's continued efforts in America to cultivate himself as a strong figure reflect his pride in his samurai heritage. His family is so used to this pride that his withered appearance when he returns from being interrogated shocks them immeasurably.

"Whatever He Did Had Flourish" establishes Papa's pride as the defining trait through which we can trace his downfall. Wakatsuki initially portrays Papa as a resourceful, adventurous, and dashing young man whose pride gives him strength of character. His pride manifests itself not only in his anger at his own father's degradation but also in the earnestness with which he lives his daily life, turning out for jobs in a brand new suit. This loving picture of Papa contrasts with Wakatsuki's later, frightening picture of him, after the war and the internment have warped his pride into misdirected anger and resentment. Papa's ultimate failure to fit in to American society is important to Wakatsuki's story because it serves as a counterpoint to Jeanne's own attempts to reconcile her Japanese ethnicity with her American identity. Papa and Jeanne's experiences differ, however, in that Jeanne's struggle leads to her eventual growth and self-realization, whereas Papa's struggle defeats him and leaves him alienated from both his family and his identity.

CHAPTERS 7–8

SUMMARY — CHAPTER 7: FORT LINCOLN: AN INTERVIEW

*When your mother and your father are having a fight,
do you want them to kill each other? Or do you just
want them to stop fighting?*

(See QUOTATIONS, p. 62)

An unnamed interrogator questions Papa at Fort Lincoln, North Dakota. The interrogator asks if he has had contact with his uncle, who is a general in Japan, but Papa says he has not. He adds that he has never returned to Japan because he is a black sheep in his family. The interrogator asks for the names of Papa's ten children, and Papa names all but Jeanne, saying there are too many to remember. The interrogator accuses him of supplying oil to a Japanese submarine off the coast of California, but Papa says only a foolish commander would voyage so far from his fleet. The interrogator shows him a photograph and asks what was in the two fifty-gallon drums seen on the deck of the Wakatsuki's boat. Papa answers that it was fish guts to attract mackerel into the nets. The interrogator asks him what he thinks of the attacks on Pearl Harbor and the American military. Papa replies that he is sad for both countries but that he is sure the Americans will win because they are bigger and richer, and Japan's leaders are stupid. He says he weeps every night for his country. The interrogator asks if he still feels loyalty to the Japanese emperor, but Papa counters by asking the interrogator's age. Papa laments that though he has been living in the United States nine years longer than the twenty-nine-year-old interrogator, he is prevented from becoming a citizen. The interrogator again asks Papa who he wants to win the war. Papa responds by asking the interrogator whether, if his mother and father were fighting, he would want them to kill each other or to just stop fighting.

SUMMARY — CHAPTER 8: INU

Papa moves into the crowded barracks with Mama and Jeanne, and does not go outside for what seems like months. Mama brings him meals from the mess halls, and he makes rice wine and brandy with extra portions of rice and canned fruit. He spends day after day getting drunk, cursing, and vomiting, and wakes up every morning moaning. Jeanne believes Papa never goes out because he feels superior to the others, but in the latrine one day she overhears some Terminal Island women whispering about Papa and using the word "*inu*." *Inu* literally means "dog" but can also refer to collaborators and informers. The women call Papa "*inu*" because he was released from Fort Lincoln earlier than the other men and is rumored to have bought his release by informing on the others.

When Mama reports the incident to Papa, he flies into a rage, cursing her for disappearing, not bringing him his food on time, and helping to spread the rumors that keep him inside the barracks all day. He threatens to kill her. Mama encourages him to strike, but when Papa raises his cane, Kiyo emerges from the bed where he has been hiding and punches Papa in the face. Papa stares at him in rage and admiration, but Kiyo runs out the door. Jeanne is proud of Kiyo but feels that everything is collapsing around her. Kiyo hides at an older sister's room for two weeks before coming to ask Papa's forgiveness. Papa accepts his apology, but Jeanne's sense of loss grows deeper as Papa continues to get drunk and abuse Mama.

ANALYSIS — CHAPTER 7

"Fort Lincoln: An Interview" is the first of three semifictional chapters that Wakatsuki uses to discuss events in her family members' lives that relate directly to the larger themes of her own experience. *Farewell to Manzanar* is primarily nonfiction, but it often includes fictional or altered details to develop its themes. Wakatsuki addresses what happened to Papa at Fort Lincoln because his struggle with being both Japanese and American mirrors her own struggle to define herself after leaving Manzanar. In later chapters, Wakatsuki admits that her father only ever uttered three or four sentences about Fort Lincoln, but she does not reveal this detail to us until after we have read the interview between Papa and the interrogator as true, word for word. This minor deception, combined with the chapter's inclusion of many biographical details found in "Whatever He Did Had Flourish," makes us forget that Wakatsuki cannot possibly be giving a wholly accurate report of her father's experience. Despite its fictional nature, "Fort Lincoln: An Interview" underscores the truths that Wakatsuki exposes throughout the work about ethnic prejudice and the difficulty of understanding one's identity.

This fictionalized interview gives us a very real and immediate sense of Papa's and the other Issei men's struggles with the impossibility of being loyal to two conflicting nations. This struggle is apparent throughout the interview, as Papa evades the interrogator's questions about his family and background. His comment that "I weep every night for my country" is ambiguous, as it is not clear whether he is referring to Japan or America. Japan is his country of birth, but America is his country of choice; in his responses he cannot commit to one side or the other because his attachments to the two, though different in nature, are equally strong. His comparison of the war between Japan and America to a quarrel between parents reveals how personal the war is to Papa. Like many Japanese Americans, he is unable to favor one country over the other, because doing so would mean rejecting either his heritage or his dream for economic and social success.

ANALYSIS — CHAPTER 8

"Inu" explores Papa's metaphor for the war between Japan and the United States as a fight between parents by looking at a real domestic dispute between Papa and Mama. Their fight is completely irrational, as Papa attacks Mama about gossip and rumors for which she is not responsible. Similarly, the war between Japan and America is an irrational byproduct of conquests and alliances taking place thousands of miles away in Europe. The children can only watch in horror as Mama invites Papa's violence, and Papa raises his cane to strike her because he is too proud to back down. Kiyo, representing the Japanese Americans who watched the war break out between their mother and father countries, strikes Papa because he "just want[s] them to stop fighting." In this way, this fight is different from the metaphorical fight between parents that Papa describes. Whereas Kiyo intervenes and cools the conflict between his parents, the Japanese Americans are unable to take action and must ultimately watch their parent countries devastate each other.

CHAPTERS 9–10

SUMMARY — CHAPTER 9: THE MESS HALL BELLS

Papa rarely talks about his experiences at Fort Lincoln because of his humiliation at being accused of disloyalty. Other men experience this sense of helplessness and rage, and these feelings eventually culminate in the December Riot, which takes place one year after the Pearl Harbor attack. In the months before the riot, the mess hall bells ring often to signal meetings to demand better food, better wages, and even outright revolt. Some meetings lead to beatings or assassination threats. On the night of December 5, 1942, a group of men attacks Fred Tayama, a leader of the Japanese American Citizens League.

The next day, the camp authorities arrest three men for the attack and send them to jail ten miles away in the town of Independence. One of the men is a cook known for trying to organize a Kitchen Worker's Union and accusing the white chief steward of selling food from the camp's warehouses on the black market. His arrest triggers a riot, but Papa refuses to participate. He keeps the family inside their barracks during the riot, and Jeanne can hear the lynch mobs roaming the camp, shouting slogans. Papa calls the rioters idiots, but Mama defends them, saying that they don't want to be treated like animals. The authorities agree to bring the cook back to camp, but by 6:00 P.M., there are 2,000 rioters and the camp security force has disappeared. One group of rioters goes to free the cook, and the other goes to the hospital to finish off Fred Tayama. One group throws rocks at a unit of military police, which responds with tear gas. The Japanese flee. In the chaos, the police open fire with machine guns, killing two Japanese and injuring ten others. Late that night the mess hall bells begin to toll, and Jeanne sees the camp searchlights for the first time. The bells toll all night and do not stop until noon the next day.

SUMMARY — CHAPTER 10: THE RESERVOIR SHACK: AN ASIDE

Jeanne's brother-in-law Kaz is foreman of a reservoir maintenance crew that must leave the camp on the night of the riots. They are issued ax handles to protect themselves if the rioters discover them cooperating with the administration. They drive to the reservoir, check the water, and set up camp in a small shack where each crew must spend its twenty-four-hour shift. Kaz, lying in his cot, thinks he sees something go past the window. Suddenly the door flies open and four military police storm into the room. They back the Japanese up against the wall at gunpoint, thinking that they have discovered a group of saboteurs. The young sergeant asks what the Japanese are doing, and Kaz explains that they are the reservoir crew and are outside camp on official orders. The sergeant is suspicious of them and asks why they have ax handles. Kaz explains that the ax handles are for protection and suggests that the sergeant go back to camp to verify the story. The reservoir crew and the military police stare at each other in fear until the sergeant returns with clearance thirty minutes later.

ANALYSIS — CHAPTER 9

"The Mess Hall Bells," one of the most violent episodes of the memoir, questions why it takes so long for riots to happen within the camps, given the inhumane living conditions. Wakatsuki depicts the Japanese as subordinate: they obey every order issued by the government and go willingly to the interrogations. There is little evidence of force on the part of the U.S. military. However, the December Riot shows that many of the Issei men were not content after having been detained in other camps. Rather than channel their anger at the oppressive forces of the U.S. government, they focus it upon each other as they rush to identify *inu*. In striking back at the *inu* they suspect of betraying them, these uprising Japanese Americans begin behaving, ironically, like dogs themselves, roaming in bands and calling for blood. They are justified in their anger, but it is difficult to sympathize with them because what they are doing to each other is as unjust and cruel as what the U.S. government has done to them.

ANALYSIS — CHAPTER 10

Until this point, fear plays a relatively minor part in Wakatsuki's story, but "The Mess Hall Bells" and "The Reservoir Shack: An Aside" focus on the buildup of fear between the Japanese and non-Japanese Americans. The events in both chapters occur at night, with one group's ill feelings about another leading to a tense confrontation. In "The Mess Hall Bells" shouting mobs roam the camp like wild dogs searching for traitors, and Jeanne, locked in her barracks by her father, can only imagine what is going on from the sound of people rushing past and gunshots. The searchlight, which Jeanne sees for the first time that night, and the haunting mess hall

bells, which toll until noon the next day in memory of the dead and
wounded, contribute to the eeriness of the scene both for us and the
characters. Similarly, in "The Reservoir Shack: An Aside," the military police's mistrust of the Japanese reservoir crew results in a
standoff between the two units. Because of fear, none of the men on
either side can communicate, and without communication, the men
can only stand frozen against the wall, staring. The fact that the two
sides can only stare at each other in silent fear shows how much fear
has become an obstacle even to simple human interaction between
whites and Japanese.

CHAPTER 11

SUMMARY — YES YES NO NO

In December the new camp director gives a Christmas tree to each
family, but Jeanne is disappointed with Christmas because of the
poor presents, the wind, and Papa's drunkenness. In February conditions worsen when the government begins to require that everyone over seventeen swear a Loyalty Oath. The oath consists of two
yes-or-no questions: the first concerns whether one is willing to
serve in the U.S. military; the second concerns whether one will
swear allegiance to the United States and renounce allegiance to
Japan.

The oath becomes a topic of debate in camp, and even Papa
emerges from his five-month isolation. He argues with the block
organizers who come to his barracks, as well as with Mama,
Granny, and Woody. Woody says he would be willing to fight, but
Papa argues that a soldier must believe in that for which he is fighting. The Japanese Americans do not know how to respond to the
Loyalty Oath. Answering "No No" will result in being shipped
back to Japan, but answering "Yes Yes" will result in being drafted
into the U.S. military. A third option, relocation, allows families to
leave camp if they have a sponsor and are willing to leave the West
Coast. The Loyalty Oath is intended to speed up the relocation
paperwork and determine which Japanese are loyal enough to serve
as soldiers in the war. Many Japanese become very anti-American,
but Papa decides to answer "Yes Yes" because he thinks America
will win the war and does not want to be sent back to Japan.

A meeting is called to discuss a collective "No No" vote, and
Papa attends even though the others will call him an "*inu*" for sup-
porting the "Yes Yes" position. At about 4:00 P.M., Jeanne is play-

ing hopscotch in the wind when she hears a commotion. She hears Papa yelling "*eta,*" meaning "trash," and she sees him tackle another man who is running out of the meeting. Papa has defended the "Yes Yes" position, and the man has called him an "*inu.*" A sandstorm arises, and back inside the barracks Papa is silent. A friend of Chizu's arrives, and she sings the Japanese national anthem, *Kimi ga yo,* with Papa, who begins to cry. Wakatsuki narrates that the national anthem, which is actually a Japanese poem from the ninth century, speaks of a small stone that becomes a massive rock covered by thousands of years of moss. In Japan, Papa's family had a stone lantern over which they poured a bucketful of water each day to keep the moss growing.

ANALYSIS

The Loyalty Oath is a psychological reflection of the physical imprisonment that the camp represents. Wakatsuki calls the Loyalty Oath a "corral"—a pen for livestock—because it pins the Japanese into a limited range of choices. Like the camps, the oath seems to the U.S. government a practical solution to the uncertainty about Japanese-American loyalty. But like the camps, the oath does not give the Japanese any satisfactory path out of their situation. They cannot fathom being deported, for it would mean returning to Japan with no home to go to, since the native Japanese would see them as enemies. Nor can they fathom declaring loyalty and being drafted, for they would be forced to fight against their own people and defend a country that has unjustly imprisoned them. The only safe option, which the government calls relocation, would release the Japanese from the camps but force them to say farewell to the West Coast and the only homes they have ever known. By forcing the Japanese to choose either "Yes Yes" or "No No," the oath leaves many of them with only one choice: to avoid the oath and try to remain in the camp.

The stone in the Japanese national anthem, *Kimi ga yo,* is a metaphor for the endurance that both Papa and the Japanese Americans as a whole show. The idea that a small stone "will grow into a massive rock" is illogical. Normally, a rock would erode over the course of thousands of years, but in the poem, the rock grows larger. In suggesting that the rock's increasing size results from the thick moss that covers it, the poem employs a logic that contrasts with the logic of the Western proverb "a rolling stone gathers no moss." The Western saying champions an idea of restlessness—by always moving and keeping active, an individual stays fresh and alive. The Japanese saying, on the other hand, celebrates growth and maturation through permanence. This idea of endurance resulting in growth recurs later, when her experiences of ethnic prejudice require Jeanne to examine her values.

Despite its symbolic significance, *Kimi ga yo* is not as innocent a song as Wakatsuki makes it out to be. In fact, many Japanese people today refuse to sing it because they see it as a relic of a past in which the emperor was worshipped like a god. The first lines of *Kimi ga yo,* which pray, "May thy peaceful reign last long / May it last for thousands of years," are a reference to the divinity of the Japanese emperor. In the ancient Shinto religion of Japan, the emperor is believed to be the direct descendent of the sun goddess. During World War II, the Japanese military leaders used the emperor as a patriotic symbol to fuel Japanese nationalism. Japan still has an emperor, though the office is removed from political affairs and is thus relatively powerless. The emperor is revered like figurehead monarchs in many countries, but the Japanese are aware of the violence that resulted from emperor-worship, and many view *Kimi ga yo* with distaste. The anthem's associations with World War II and the history of the Japanese empire taint the anthem's poetic content, no matter how appropriate it is to Wakatsuki's analysis of Japanese character.

CHAPTERS 12–13

SUMMARY — CHAPTER 12: MANZANAR, U.S.A.

In the spring of 1943, the Wakatsuki family moves to nicer barracks in Block 28 near one of the old pear orchards. Wakatsuki tells us that the Spanish word *manzanar* means "apple orchard" and that there were once many orchards in Owens Valley, where Manzanar is located. Papa tends the fruit trees, and Mama is closer to the hospital where she works as a dietician. Their new lodgings are twice the size of their old ones and have ceilings and linoleum floors. Papa continues to distill liquor, but he drinks less because he spends more time outdoors. After the first year, the Japanese are allowed to venture outside the fence for recreation, and Papa goes on hikes, looking for driftwood, which he carves into furniture. He also paints, sketches, and even builds a rock garden outside the Wakatsuki barracks, with stepping stones leading up to the door.

Life in camp becomes subdued and *shikata ga nai,* "it cannot be helped," again becomes the motto. Many families plant gardens, the

administration begins to operate a farm, and some former professional gardeners build a small park. Manzanar becomes its own
world with its own churches, stores, movie theaters, and schools,
and many of its residents forget about the war. Papa talks Woody
out of volunteering for the military, and Woody works at the general
store while he waits to be drafted. Kiyo collects arrowheads
unearthed by the strong winds and sells them to old men, and Ray
plays on a local football team. Jeanne's older sister, Lillian, joins a
hillbilly band called the Sierra Stars. Jeanne's oldest brother, Bill,
leads a dance band called the Jive Bombers, singing such hits as
Don't Fence Me In. There is a picture of the band in the Manzanar
High School 1943–1944 yearbook, *Our World,* along with photos
of cheerleaders and the school play, whose description reads "the
story of a typical American home." The last two photos in the yearbook show a watchtower and a woman with her dog walking down
a peaceful path outside of camp.

SUMMARY—OUTINGS, EXPLORATIONS
The camp authorities create a high school and elementary school,
and Jeanne enrolls in fourth grade. Her teacher is a spinster from
Kentucky, but Jeanne says she is the best teacher she has ever had.
Jeanne also joins the Glee Club, which gives concerts throughout
the camp. The War Relocation Department brings in leaders, mostly
Quakers, to run a recreation program. On weekends the leaders
organize hiking trips to the recently built campgrounds in the hills
outside of camp. One leader, a Quaker girl named Lois, has a crush
on a Japanese boy, and the two arrange an overnight camping trip
for the younger girls in order to spend time together. Jeanne enjoys
the occasional excursions but is afraid of spending too much time
outside the compound.

Jeanne begins taking baton-twirling lessons, practices for
months, and eventually joins the baton club at school. Wakatsuki
wonders why she was so attracted to such an all-American activity
and compares it to her experience taking Japanese dance lessons
from an old geisha—a Japanese woman trained to entertain men—
in camp. The geisha teaches traditional *odori* dancing to young girls
who want to participate in the *obon* festival honoring dead ances-
tors, but Jeanne does not understand the geisha's traditional attitudes and Japanese dialect. Two girls in the class tell Jeanne that a
good dancer must use hair tonic on her face, put cold cream in her
hair, and never wear underpants, but Mama tells her the girls are

teasing. Jeanne also tries taking ballet lessons, but she is unimpressed by the out-of-shape teacher and her *daikon ashi,* which refers to horseradish-shaped legs. Disappointed, Jeanne returns to her study of religion with the nuns and longs to be baptized in a white gown and veil. When she announces her intention to Papa, he gets angry and refuses her wishes on the grounds that she will be unable to marry a Japanese boy. One of the nuns is a friend of Papa's and tries to reason with him, but he says Jeanne is too young. Jeanne decides she hates Papa and returns to baton twirling.

ANALYSIS — MANZANAR, U.S.A.

Part II of *Farewell to Manzanar* opens with the Wakatsuki family's move to the new barracks next to the orchard, underscoring that the move marks a new phase in Jeanne's family life. The fruit trees symbolize fertility and rejuvenation, and the move to the fruit orchard coincides with a return to a more normal family life. Though he still indulges in alcohol, Papa becomes productive, tending the orchard and pursuing creative interests such as carving furniture out of driftwood. Similarly, Jeanne and her sisters begin to busy themselves with various activities and hobbies. Additionally, the Wakatsukis' residence is much more inhabitable than their previous one. For the first time since the memoir's opening moments, the Wakatsuki family is planted. As each family member becomes involved in his or her own interests, the family becomes less and less a source of tension.

The mainstream American nature of the lives the Japanese Americans re-create for themselves within the confines of Manzanar reminds us that these prisoners are loyal American citizens. Manzanar is an all-American town, and through the parade of typical American cultural phenomena such as touch football teams, yearbooks, jive bands, and school dances, Wakatsuki once again raises the question of how American and how Japanese the Japanese Americans really are. The young Nisei are responsible for most of the American aspects of camp life, and their enthusiasm for American culture demonstrates how the Japanese are becoming more and more American with each generation. The name of Bill's dance band, "the Jive Bombers," for example, is an obvious pun on the term for Japanese kamikaze pilots famous for dive-bombing their targets. This lighthearted reference to these pilots shows that Bill feels little, if any, sympathy for the Japanese military effort. Additionally, he sings *Don't Fence Me In* not because he wants to protest against the camps but because it is a hit song in the United States, and he wants his band to be up to date. That Bill does not even recognize how politically appropriate the song's words are to his situation underscores how little he feels that he is a victim of injustice rather than just an ordinary American.

ANALYSIS—OUTINGS, EXPLORATIONS

Jeanne's mild fear at venturing outside of camp shows that even though the camp is a prison to her, it provides a security that puts her at peace with herself. Her first timid attempts at discovering her true self result in disappointment, as she is uncomfortable exploring beyond what is known and certain. The camp is her entire world, and there are enough things for a young child to explore in the camp without the complication of venturing outside. But the limited scope of her explorations and her choice of such non-Japanese activities as ballet, baton twirling, and religious study suggest that in discovering her own identity, Jeanne will eventually have to reconcile these American tendencies with her Japanese ancestry. She gravitates to American activities because being American is all she has ever known. But when she is finally pushed out of the comfort of the camp, she has the deeper realization that in order to understand her identity, her definition of herself must go beyond simply being Japanese or American and must address what it means to be both at the same time.

CHAPTERS 14, 15 & 16

SUMMARY—CHAPTER 14: IN THE FIREBREAK

In her later life, Wakatsuki concedes that Papa was right to protest her being baptized at a young age. At the time of his refusal, however, Jeanne cannot forgive him and feels herself drifting farther and farther away from him. Jeanne's oldest sister, Eleanor, has returned to the camp because her husband has been drafted, and she is in the camp hospital giving birth. The family is worried because two of Jeanne's older sisters hemorrhaged badly during childbirth, and blood plasma is in short supply. One sister was saved by a blood transfusion from Woody, but the other bled to death. Eleanor is in her second day of labor, and Mama and Papa take turns sitting with her. On the afternoon of the second day, Mama runs across the firebreak, a patch of cleared land, shouting for Papa. Papa is afraid and runs to meet her, but the news is good: Eleanor has given birth to a boy. Both Mama and Papa begin to cry, but Jeanne is strangely detached. She feels invisible as she watches her parents talk tenderly to each other in the middle of the firebreak.

SUMMARY—CHAPTER 15: DEPARTURES

Mama and Papa become even closer in the following months, but like many of the other Japanese, most of the older Wakatsuki children decide to relocate or join the military. By 1944, only 6,000 people remain in the camp, and most are children or elderly persons. Eleanor moves back to Reno and stays with friends. Woody is drafted in August 1944, and despite Papa's suggestion that he refuse to serve, he reports for duty when his unit is called up in November. The whole family goes to see him off, and although Jeanne does not understand where he is going, she feels the way she did when the FBI took Papa away. Jeanne remembers the day they waved goodbye to the fleet on the wharf in San Pedro Harbor, but now there are 500 other proud Japanese waving goodbye. The all-Nisei 442nd Combat Regiment that Woody joins is famous for its valor in Europe, and one mother in camp has recently received a Congressional Medal of Honor for a son killed in Italy. As more and more families are split up by the departures, people begin to worry about what will happen to them after the war.

SUMMARY—CHAPTER 16: FREE TO GO

In December 1944, in the last of three cases brought against the camps, the Supreme Court rules that the camps are illegal. The first case is brought by a Nisei university student, Gordon Hirabayashi, who violated the curfew imposed in 1942, but the Supreme Court upholds the War Department's restrictions on the movements of the Japanese. The second case is brought by Fred Korematsu, who evaded the removal to Manzanar and underwent plastic surgery in order to stay with his white girlfriend. Korematsu's case protests the fact that no German Americans or Italian Americans were relocated, but again the Supreme Court rules in favor of the army's evacuation policy. The third suit is brought by a twenty-one-year-old Nisei named Mitsue Endo, who challenges the legality of the government's detaining loyal citizens against their will. The Supreme Court is forced to decide in her favor, and the army, anticipating the decision, announces that it will close the camps in the next twelve months.

The Japanese response to the decision is far from joyful, as many of Manzanar's inhabitants have no homes to which to return, and wartime propaganda has turned public opinion against them. Prejudiced groups such as No Japs Incorporated and The Pacific Coast

Japanese Problem League even try to block Japanese resettlement on the West Coast. Many Japanese fear leaving the camps, but the government insists that the camps close. Most Japanese have few problems resettling, but rumors of attacks on returning Japanese fuel the fears of those remaining in camp. Jeanne is confused because she has always associated the world outside with good things like the Sears, Roebuck catalogue. Now, however, she begins to prepare herself for what was once just an unnamed ache: being hated. Most of the older Wakatsuki children move to New Jersey, though they all realize that Papa will never move back east. Jeanne compares him to a freed black slave who does not know what to do with his freedom because slavery is all he has ever known.

SUMMARY & ANALYSIS

ANALYSIS—CHAPTER 14

In "In the Firebreak," Wakatsuki uses the firebreak as a symbol of the end of her parents' fighting. The firebreak is a wide swath of empty land intended to prevent fire from spreading from one part of camp to another. The birth of their grandson, which Mama and Papa celebrate in the firebreak, is a sort of symbolic firebreak, preventing a conflict that has been brewing since Papa nearly struck Mama with his cane. The image of Mama running breathlessly toward a stumbling Papa across the openness of the windswept sand represents the psychological distance that Mama and Papa must cross to come together again. Jeanne comments that Papa's and her fear that Mama would bring bad news must have slowed Mama down. This thought illustrates that it was not actual conflict but simply the unspoken fear they coped with on a daily basis that kept Mama and Papa from reconciling their differences.

ANALYSIS—CHAPTER 15

The departures of the older Wakatsuki children, particularly Woody, represent the breakdown taking place within the family. Woody is earlier a surrogate father for the younger children during Papa's absence, and his decision to accept being drafted into military service distances him from his family, especially from Papa. Papa is unable to declare loyalty to either Japan or the United States at Fort Lincoln and supports the "Yes Yes" position on the Loyalty Oath only as a practical measure. Woody, on the other hand, is fully loyal to the United States and is willing to die for his country. He does not care that the same government that has kept him imprisoned for the last two years is now asking for his help. Along with the other members of his all-Nisei regiment, he feels he must do his duty as an American citizen. Papa's struggle with being a noncitizen makes him fearful of the outside world, but Woody can leave the camp because he is sure of himself and his right to a place in America. Unfortunately for the family, however, Woody's strength in the face of adversity is what has kept the family together, and his departure begins the final stage of the family's deterioration.

ANALYSIS — CHAPTER 16
The Supreme Court's delay in ruling against the internment policy is a reflection of the political and cultural atmosphere in America during the 1940s. The Civil Rights Act, which prohibits discrimination based on color, race, religion, or national origin, was not enacted until 1964, and in the 1940s there was little precedent for establishing the illegality of ethnic discrimination. The first two cases that Wakatsuki mentions were doomed from the beginning because they addressed only the issue of ethnic prejudice, which the courts had never really dealt with before. The Endo case, however, was successful because it eliminated ethnic prejudice from the equation. Endo built her case on the Constitutional principle of habeas corpus, which allows a judge to demand the release of a citizen imprisoned without cause. Endo had signed the Loyalty Oath, and by petitioning for habeas corpus, she asserted her Constitutional right to freedom and forced the Supreme Court to decide in her favor. Because of the air of fear and intolerance in America during World War II, it took one of the oldest American legal precedents to correct the hypocrisy of the United States' policy of imprisoning its own loyal citizens.

CHAPTER 17

SUMMARY — IT IS ALL STARTING OVER
In June 1945, the schools close and the high school produces a final yearbook, *Valediction 1945,* bearing a photo of a hand squeezing pliers on a length of barbed wire. Cultivation of the farm stops, and the administration auctions off the equipment. The army announces that the camps will close by December 1, and families who do not leave will be scheduled for resettlement, either to a place of their choosing or to their former communities. Papa is stubborn and chooses to let the government arrange for the Wakatsuki family's resettlement. His boats are gone, and a new law has made it illegal

for Issei to hold commercial fishing licenses. He spends his time reading the news of the war and relocation with disgust.

Papa and Mama regret not leaving sooner because there is no more housing available, and Mama's friend says that the difficulties the Japanese Americans experienced when they were evacuated in 1942 are starting again. Jeanne's parents argue about who is to blame. Mama asks Jeanne for a back massage, but Papa insists that he give it. Mama has not seen a doctor because there are too many patients, and she repeats her friend's comment that it is like 1942 all over again. Wakatsuki notes that the barracks are slowly being deserted and that the moss in Papa's rock garden has dried out. Papa reports that block leaders are petitioning the administration to keep the camp open until everyone has a place to stay. He plans to ask the government for a loan so that he can organize a cooperative of returning Japanese to build a housing project. He feels the government owes it to returning Japanese, but neither he nor Mama have much hope for the plan's success.

On August 6, 1945, the United States drops an atomic bomb on Hiroshima, ending the war and any hopes of staying in the camps. The newspapers print photos of the mushroom cloud over Hiroshima, but few people realize the magnitude of what has happened. A week later, Americans dance in the street at the news of the Japanese surrender, and Japanese in the camps rejoice that they are no longer the enemy. Papa reflects on his now-departed children and his family in Hiroshima. As busloads of people leave the camp, Papa continues reading the newspaper and waiting for his turn to leave the camp, which finally comes in October 1945.

ANALYSIS

The title of the final Manzanar High School yearbook, *Valediction 1945,* highlights the different reactions the Issei and Nisei have to the closing of the camps. A valediction is an act of saying farewell, and the yearbook's opening photo of pliers about to cut through barbed wire shows that the young adults are ready to say farewell to Manzanar in a way that the 6,000 elderly and children who remained are not. Throughout the memoir, the Issei tell themselves that the camp must be endured, but their appeal to the administration to stay in camp longer shows how much their acceptance of the camp has made them dependent on its support. Wakatsuki's image of her father staring at the mountains to calm his thoughts recalls her earlier comparison of him to a freed slave and reiterates the difficulties experienced by Issei in trying to adjust to normal life outside the camps. Whereas the Nisei can at least be confident in their citizenship, the internment has torn up the fragile roots the Issei planted before the war. Homeless, jobless, and without property, the Issei cannot say farewell to Manzanar as easily as the Nisei, because to leave the security of the camp means to face a society that has no place for them.

The idea of starting over that Mama's friend mentions and that Mama mournfully repeats has a double meaning that refers to the difficulty of life outside the camp. By "It is all starting over," Mama means that the Japanese will once again have to face the same difficulties they experienced in moving to the camps. The deeper meaning for the Issei, however, is that they must start their entire lives over, but that this time the odds are stacked against them. When the Issei arrived during the prewar boom years, jobs and housing were plentiful. By 1944, however, over a million people had moved to the West Coast to fill jobs created by the war industry or vacated by relocated Japanese Americans. Papa's naïve and doomed plan for a Japanese-American cooperative housing project shows how desperate the Issei have become. After years of mistreatment, they still believe that the government must help them start over. This help, however, never comes, and the reality of postwar unemployment and discrimination soon puts an end to their hopes.

The camp's state of stagnation and neglect at the end of the internment mirrors the situation the Japanese find themselves in when forced to leave. Just as the departing Japanese must try to overcome the same difficulties they face at the beginning of the internment, the Manzanar camp itself returns to the dilapidated state in which the Japanese find it in 1942. Papa's rock garden, in which the moss is now dry, recalls the image from the Japanese national anthem, *Kimi ga yo,* of the rock growing large with moss. The withered, untended rock garden suggests that simple endurance is not enough and that even the most enduring of rocks need care if they are to grow. Even though the Japanese have survived the camps, their stoic acceptance of camp life has left them unprepared for and fearful of what lies ahead.

SUMMARY & ANALYSIS

CHAPTERS 18–19

SUMMARY—CHAPTER 18: KA-KE, NEAR HIROSHIMA: APRIL 1946

Woody visits Papa's family outside of Hiroshima nearly a year after the atomic bomb is dropped, and Toyo, his great-aunt, shows him a graveyard where the gravestones are tilted from the bomb blast. One member of the family has been lost, but Toyo does not want to talk about it. She explains that she has brought Woody to the grave-yard to show him where his father was buried in 1913. Woody pro-tests that his father is still alive and well in California, but Toyo explains that when the family had no word from him for nine years, they decided he was dead and placed a gravestone for him in the graveyard. She says her happiness at hearing that he is alive has erased the trauma that the war put her through.

Woody has been afraid to visit his father's family in Hiroshima because he is an American Nisei and part of the occupying American army. Finally, however, he decides to go bearing a gift of fifty pounds of sugar, which is in short supply due to inflated black market prices. His family immediately sees past his American haircut and smile, and sees only that he is his father's son. They accept him instantly and welcome his gift with only slight embarrassment. The family's elegant country house is bare except for a few mats and an altar, but Toyo bears herself with dignity. They eat a special meal on nice por-celain, drink precious sake, and Woody sleeps under their finest bed-ding. He is proud to discover that Papa's stories of his family's nobility are true and imagines that Papa would be proud of how they received Woody.

Just as he is falling asleep, he feels a presence near him. It is Toyo, kneeling beside him and crying. She says he looks just like Papa, she and quickly leaves. Woody conjures up an image of Papa and is amazed at the resemblance between Papa and Toyo. In seeing her, he understands Papa's pride and wishes he had asked Toyo about him. He decides to ask her the next day and to climb the hill Papa used to climb.

SUMMARY—CHAPTER 19: RE-ENTRY

A few days before leaving Manzanar, Papa decides that the family must leave in style. Despite Mama's protests, he walks to the nearby town of Lone Pine to buy a car. Papa prefers unique cars and returns with a midnight blue Nash sedan with a dashboard gearshift. It takes Papa four days and three trips to transport the remaining nine members of the family back to Long Beach. The car breaks down nearly every hundred miles, but Papa always manages to fix it. Jeanne compares the overpacked car to an Oklahoma family moving west during the Great Depression. Papa drinks all the way back to Los Angeles but sobers up just before entering the city, as if he is waiting for an attack. Jeanne is afraid of the word "*hate*," which she has heard her family using, and imagines hate as a black cloud descending on her. But when they enter the city, there is no sign of hatred, and it seems as if nothing has changed. Jeanne compares the trip home to a trip through a time machine.

There is little housing available to the 60,000 returning Japanese, and the Wakatsukis have a hard time finding a place to live. The American Friends Service helps them find a three-bedroom apartment at the Cabrillo Homes housing project in Long Beach. For the first time in three years, they have a kitchen and toilet, but most of the family furniture has disappeared from storage, and Papa's fishing boats are nowhere to be found. Papa maintains hope by clinging to his plan for a Japanese housing collective, and Mama goes to work in a cannery to support the family because Papa is too proud to take such a job. Jeanne's fear of the dark cloud of hatred slowly recedes.

ANALYSIS — CHAPTER 18

Woody's visit to Hiroshima, though semifictional, is an important window into understanding Papa's character and the origin of the Wakatsuki pride that is so prominent in *Farewell to Manzanar*. The Japanese Wakatsuki family has been just as destroyed as the American Wakatsuki family, but the Japanese Wakatsukis have been buoyed up by what Woody sees as "an ancient, inextinguishable dignity." Where Toyo's dignity seems to raise her stature and paint her in a tragic light, Papa's stubborn pride only makes him seem pathetic. Toyo and the others receive Woody with utmost hospitality, even though he is part of an occupying army that has recently decimated their country. In comparison, Papa's bouts of hostility toward his family during their time at Manzanar are undignified and shameful. Woody comes to understand that he, Aunt Toyo, and Papa all share the same Wakatsuki pride, but in each of them it takes a different form because they have each gone through different circumstances.

ANALYSIS — CHAPTER 19

In "Re-entry," Wakatsuki uses imagery from science fiction to highlight the contrast between the changed Japanese Americans and the seemingly unchanged outside world. The term "re-entry" refers to the return of a spacecraft from outer space into Earth's atmosphere. Wakatsuki's use of this word to describe her return to Los Angeles gives the sense that she is returning from a far-off planet rather than a valley 200 miles away. This alien world she expects to encounter is dominated by hate, and her conception of hate as a "dark, amorphous cloud" suggests that she believes hate is a sort of supernatural event rather than a human reaction. Additionally, her feeling of having voyaged in a time machine back to the same life she left before the internment implies the years at Manzanar have suddenly ceased to exist. Wakatsuki's suggestion that the Japanese are expected to continue as though the war years have been erased is tragic, however, for their experiences during the war have caused changes in them that are too important to forget.

The difficulty of understanding one's identity is one of the themes of *Farewell to Manzanar,* and Jeanne's story demonstrates the obstacles to self-discovery. Papa is eventually able to understand Woody's American roots, and Woody comes to understand Papa's Japanese dignity, but Jeanne must come to terms with her own identity at the same time that she must face the prejudice of postwar America. Her departure from the camp marks an acceleration of the process of self-discovery she begins at Manzanar, a process that climaxes in her experiences with prejudice after the war and comes to a resolution when she later visits the camp and begins writing her memoir. The reexamination of her own story in *Farewell to Manzanar* is a means for Wakatsuki to understand the erased years of her time at Manzanar and how they shaped the person she has become.

CHAPTER 20

SUMMARY — A DOUBLE IMPULSE

> *I was suddenly aware of what being of Japanese ancestry was going to be like. I would be seen as someone foreign, or as someone other than American, or perhaps not be seen at all.*
>
> *(See* QUOTATIONS, *p. 63)*

Jeanne enters sixth grade and finds her teacher warm and kind. When she is asked to read aloud and does so, however, the children stare, and one girl, Radine, comments that she didn't know Jeanne could speak English. Jeanne is stunned that the girl can doubt her ability to speak English and suddenly realizes that having a Japanese face will not cause people to attack her but will simply make people see her as foreign. She begins to wish she could become invisible. She blames the wartime deportation of 110,000 Japanese on both white society's inability to see Japanese people as individuals and the Japanese acceptance of this attitude. Her desire to disappear conflicts with her need to be accepted, and she becomes involved in academics, sports, and student government. Outside of school, however, Jeanne learns that she cannot be friends with certain children because their parents will not accept her. Jeanne takes this rejection quietly, but is dissatisfied with her school activities. She asks Radine if she can join the Girl Scouts, but Radine's mother, who is assistant troop leader, will not allow her to do so.

Jeanne does not blame Radine for her mother's reaction, and the two become close friends. Radine even stands up for Jeanne in public. Jeanne teaches Radine how to twirl a baton and imagines herself as a majorette leading a band. In the fall, the two girls audition to be baton twirlers for a local Boy Scouts drum and bugle corps, and both are accepted. Jeanne is made majorette and leads the band in a white outfit with a gold braid. She soon realizes that her acceptance in the Boy Scouts band is partly because the boys and their fathers like to see young girls performing in tight outfits and short skirts. She learns that her sexuality is a tool she can use to gain acceptance.

Woody and Ray come back on leave from the military, and though they tease Jeanne about her skinny legs, which they call *"gobo ashi,"* they are actually quite proud of her. Papa does not share their pride and wants Jeanne to become more Japanese. His housing project has failed, and Jeanne has lost respect for him because they are still in the cramped apartment where they must eat in shifts. Papa tries to fish for abalone with Woody off the coast of Mexico, but the enterprise fails when worms attack the drying fish. Papa begins to rely on Woody, who has grown in stature since his visit to Japan and who, as a citizen, can easily cross borders and obtain fishing licenses. Jeanne loses even more respect for Papa because of his continual heavy drinking and refusal to conform to American ways. At a PTA awards dinner, he embarrasses Jeanne by overdressing and bowing to the gathered crowd of parents in Japanese fashion. Jeanne begins to see him as unforgivably foreign.

ANALYSIS

Throughout *Farewell to Manzanar*, Wakatsuki depicts herself as a naïve child to show that it is primarily her youth that prevents her from truly understanding the motives behind the internment. She often uses childlike images and simple incidents to describe abstract concepts or large events, such as the image of the returning fleet of ships as a flock of seagulls that she uses in the first chapter to relate the bombing of Pearl Harbor. Here she uses the wonderment at her ability to speak English to pinpoint the moment at which she realizes that she is no longer a child. *Farewell to Manzanar* is a coming-of-age story, but unlike most coming-of-age stories, the growing up occurs quite quickly and is as abrupt as the trip through the time machine she imagines upon returning from Manzanar. There is no transition for her into the world outside Manzanar, and the shock of realizing that she "will be seen as something foreign, or as someone other than American, or perhaps not be seen at all," strips her of her innocence. Radine's simple but prejudiced comment makes Jeanne feel shame for the first time and initiates her into how people really see her as a Japanese American.

Wakatsuki uses the concept of invisibility to discuss both the origin of ethnic prejudice and her own specific experiences. Her suggestion that the internment of 110,000 Japanese is a result of Americans' inability to see beyond the "slant-eyed face" is one of the rare moments in her memoir that she places blame on white people. However, she also blames her own people's acceptance of this invisibility. Jeanne too begins to accept her fate, but her desire to make her Japanese face disappear conflicts with her need to be accepted as an American and as an individual, and accounts for the chapter's title, "A Double Impulse." The paradox of this double impulse connects her to Papa's struggle with being Japanese in America. But Papa is beaten down by ethnic prejudice and resorts to drinking; Jeanne fights it by choosing the areas in which it is acceptable for her to succeed, such as extracurricular activities and academics. Though ultimately unsatisfying, her involvement in academics and school activities are an important first step in countering her invisibility and coming to terms with her own identity.

Jeanne grows more distant from Papa after leaving the camp not because she has lost respect for him but because he rejects her attempts to fit into American life. Papa's alcoholism, refusal to work, and misfortunes with his housing project make him pathetic and nearly unlikable, but his inability to understand Jeanne's need to be accepted creates the widest gap between them. At the beginning of *Farewell to Manzanar*, Papa seems to embrace America and shun Japan, so much so that he has given all but two of his children American names. His experience with prejudice, however, has disillusioned him and made him resentful. Jeanne's feeling that Papa wants her to be "Miss Hiroshima 1904," the year of his departure from Japan, suggests that Papa has nearly given up on America and is yearning to return to his Japanese roots. It is sad that Jeanne, who is so afraid of being seen as foreign, begins to see her father as "unforgivably a foreigner." In striving to be accepted in a world where being Japanese is a handicap, she is unable to see beyond her own father's Japanese identity and tries instead to make him disappear from her life.

CHAPTER 21

SUMMARY — THE GIRL OF MY DREAMS

> *I feel no malice toward this girl. Watching, I am simply emptied, and in the dream I want to cry out, because she is something I can never be.*
>
> *(See* QUOTATIONS, *p. 64)*

Jeanne shuns Papa's Japanese ancestry and embraces her friendship with Radine. Radine's parents are poor whites from Texas, and growing up together in an ethically mixed ghetto, Radine and Jeanne are almost socially equal and become best friends. Their relationship changes, however, when they move to Long Beach Polytechnic High School. Radine is asked to join sororities from which Jeanne is barred. Boys flirt with Jeanne but always ask Radine to the dances instead. The harshest blow is that Radine is promoted to song girl in the band, while the band teacher must fight with the administration even to name Jeanne majorette. Jeanne is demoralized by Radine's success because she knows the two of them share so many qualities, even their taste in boys. Jeanne is ashamed that her Japanese face and Japanese father prevent her from dating the boys she likes, but she does not want to change her face. She wants to be accepted. She begins to have recurring dreams about a blonde, blue-eyed girl being admired in a room full of people as she, Jeanne, watches through a window. Jeanne loses interest in school, begins hanging out on the streets, and considers dropping out.

One day, Papa nearly kills himself when he gets drunk on whiskey and homemade wine, and he finally gives up drinking to begin farming again. In 1951 he moves the family to the Santa Clara Valley outside of San Jose and begins sharecropping a hundred acres for a strawberry farmer. Jeanne is a senior in high school, but she tries to start over in the new school. The following spring, her homeroom nominates her to be carnival queen. On election day, instead of dressing like a typical 1950s bobbysoxer, Jeanne dresses in an exotic sarong with her hair down and a hibiscus flower behind her ear. The applause and cheers indicate that she will win by a landslide, but her friend Leonard Rodriguez, who helps out in the office, reports that the teachers are trying to stuff the ballot box to prevent her from winning. Jeanne is afraid to confront them, but Leonard does it for her, exposing the teachers and saving Jeanne's victory.

Papa is angry that Jeanne has won, and even angrier that she used her sexuality to entice white boys. He is worried about how American Jeanne has become and afraid that she will end up marrying a white boy, so he forces her to take Japanese dance lessons at a Buddhist temple in exchange for permitting her to be the carnival queen. She quits after only ten lessons, but as a compromise, she decides to wear a conservative dress for the coronation ceremony instead of one of the strapless dresses that other girls are wearing. On coronation night, the other girls compliment Jeanne on her dress, but when she enters the gym, the crowd begins to murmur. Jeanne feels uncomfortable in her dress and realizes her mistake in trying to be someone she is not. She understands that her Japanese face will still keep her from being invited to the white girls' reception after the ceremony, and she begins to wonder who she really is.

ANALYSIS

That Jeanne is more hurt by Radine's successes than by ethnic prejudice shows that she is searching for a deeper kind of acceptance. She is prepared for the prejudice that keeps her from being song girl but not prepared for how anti-Japanese prejudice drives a wedge between her and Radine, whom she thinks of as a social equal. Their common economic background and similar tastes make it painful for Jeanne to watch Radine's rise, for she wants, but is denied, the same thing for herself. When the boys who flirt with Jeanne ask Radine to the dances instead, Jeanne is forced to admit that prejudice is more powerful even than love and friendship. After such a realization, it is not surprising that Jeanne withdraws from school life and considers dropping out. Her academic and extracurricular achievements are only a mask for her deeper need for acceptance on a human level, and when hope of such acceptance is removed, there is little hope at all.

Jeanne's recurring dream of looking in at the carnival queen from outside symbolizes her inability to attain the ideal of acceptance to which she aspires. The blonde, beautiful, and adored girl in the dream is the stereotype of the American prom queen. Jeanne's separation by a window from her ideal of beauty mirrors her situation in real life, where she is allowed to watch Radine's successes but never allowed to achieve them herself. She does not envy the girl but says she is "simply emptied," showing that the dream is less a remnant of hope than a symbol of her loss and disillusionment. That this dream haunts Wakatsuki even as she writes her memoir shows that even though she has come to terms with the internment, she still struggles to reconcile her Japanese heritage with the American culture in which she grew up.

Jeanne's realization that she cannot define herself as only Japanese or only American marks the climax of her memoir. The main conflict of her story is her struggle to reconcile the Japanese and American aspects of her identity. She continually deceives herself into thinking that if she acts American, people will see past her Japanese face. She fails to understand, however, that her problem lies in defining herself not according to who she really is but according to how she wants other people to see her. It is not until she finally gains the acceptance she desires and is on display for everyone to see and judge that Jeanne finally realizes her error. The lukewarm reaction to her conservative dress at the carnival queen coronation ceremony makes her realize that neither the overly conservative version nor the overly sexualized version of herself is real. Rather, they are simply attempts to define herself according to other people's standards. This realization marks the end of her childhood naïveté and leads her to conclude that the first step in being accepted by others is for her to accept who she really is: a Japanese American.

CHAPTER 22

SUMMARY — TEN THOUSAND VOICES

Papa's life ended at Manzanar . . . . Until this trip I had not been able to admit that my own life really began there. (See QUOTATIONS, p. 65)

Jeanne is the first of her family to graduate from college and the first to marry a non-Japanese person. That most Japanese do not talk about Manzanar and that many non-Japanese have never heard of it make her wonder if she imagined the whole thing. Her family rarely talks about the camp, and some experiences remain secret, such as when an old woman spat on Jeanne and Kiyo and called them "dirty Japs." In 1966, Jeanne meets a white photographer who had worked at Manzanar, and though at first she finds it difficult, she soon begins to talk about the camp with the woman.

In April 1972, Jeanne and her husband visit the ruins of Manzanar with their three children. She is surprised that Manzanar could be located so near a highway filled with bikers and vacationers headed for the mountains. They finally spot the stand of elms and fruit trees that mark the ruins of the camp. During the internment, Manzanar was the largest town between Reno and Los Angeles, but now only a few buildings remain. Inside the camp, they notice a white obelisk marking twelve graves. Jeanne thinks of her mother, who died seven years earlier, and begins to feel and hear the presence of those who once lived at Manzanar. They explore the site and discover small rock gardens created by Issei men like her father. They also discover the remains of a small park, which ends suddenly in tumbleweeds and a bare mound.

Jeanne looks at the ruins as she would an archeological site and notices the outlines and patterns of a city. She finds a ring of stones where the American flag was raised each morning, but she is disturbed that the date on the inscription is marked A.D., as if the mason intended his work to endure for centuries. She crosses the windy firebreak, and with the wind, the sound of the voices grows. She closes her eyes and imagines that nothing has changed. She hears laughter and the singing of the Glee Club, and sees old men burning orange peels to keep away mosquitoes. She looks for the site of her former home in Block 28 and locates the orchard next to which her family used to live.

Jeanne watches her eleven-year-old daughter, who is the same age Jeanne was when the camps closed. She realizes that her life really began at the camp, just as Papa's life ended there. Since leaving the camp, she has nearly succeeded in suppressing her memory of it, but she occasionally hears her mother's voice saying that the difficulty is starting over. Now that she has visited Manzanar, she no longer wants to lose it but feels she can finally say "farewell" to it.

Just before leaving, Jeanne uncovers a stepping-stone next to a small rock garden. She imagines it is the garden Papa built and sees an image of him sitting on the porch tending to Mama's sore back. She sees a wildness in his eyes that takes her back to the day he bought the car to move the family back to Los Angeles. He is drunk and driving the car on two flat tires. He makes Mama and the girls get in the car and speeds around the camp, swerving and yelling at the departing families not to miss their bus. Jeanne is afraid, but she takes comfort in Papa's madness and suddenly has complete faith that he will get them past the dark cloud of hatred that awaits them in the outside world.

ANALYSIS

Wakatsuki's change of tone from observational to nostalgic illustrates her own transition from denying her time at Manzanar to accepting it as one of the most important events of her life. She opens the chapter with a dry, observational list of details about what she sees and hears. However, this tone takes on an eerie quality halfway through the chapter when Wakatsuki discovers the memorial to the dead and begins to hear what she thinks are the voices of ghosts of those who died in the camp. Surrounded by barbed wire, the memorial becomes a miniature image of the camp itself from which the residents cannot escape even in death. That Jeanne has almost convinced herself over the years that she only imagined Manzanar requires her to prove to herself that it is indeed real. She portrays the voices and images that come back to her as if she is reliving them. By interweaving her memories among the details of what she actually sees, she draws us into her past. By the end of the chapter, her real observations of the ruins have disappeared, and the world of her memory has completely enveloped us. Recognizing Manzanar as a real place with a real history makes Jeanne realize that her life really began there, which transforms her experience at Manzanar from an emotional burden she carries with her into a crucial part of her identity.

The visit to Manzanar is a way for Wakatsuki to reclaim what she lost when her family fell apart in the camp. In her stroll through the ruins and through her memories, she searches for signs of her family and Papa, both of which the camp destroyed, in order to restore her memory of what was good in them. The sign she finally finds is a memory of Papa's final proud and defiant ride through camp in his car. Like Woody, Jeanne comes to understand through a memory of Papa that his stubborn pride was really just a corrupted version of the flourish that had always been his greatest strength. His flourish is what she remembers most about him before the evacuation, so it is appropriate that she returns to Manzanar, where this dignity was lost, to reclaim her family's pride. For Jeanne, coming to terms with Manzanar means coming to terms with what it took from her and those she loved.

Wakatsuki's memoir focuses on the endurance of memory rather than on the ability to leave experiences behind. Though the title *Farewell to Manzanar* implies that Wakatsuki uses the act of writing this memoir to leave the camp behind, the final scene illustrates that the time she spent in the camp will always remain with her. Wakatsuki ends the novel not with a description of her life after her time at Manzanar but with a reminiscence from her camp days. In this section, she uses stones to exemplify this endurance of memory and experience. Some of the few physical reminders of the camp's existence, the precisely placed stones and concrete slabs, act as a testament to Wakatsuki that the events at Manzanar actually occurred. Like the stones, Wakatsuki's memories persist over time. She cannot simply bid the camp farewell and forget about her time there, because her experiences there helped shaped who she is.

Important Quotations Explained

1. [Mama] would quickly subordinate her own desires to those of the family or the community, because she knew cooperation was the only way to survive. At the same time she placed a high premium on personal privacy, respected it in others and insisted upon it for herself. ... Almost everyone at Manzanar had inherited this pair of traits from the generations before them who had learned to live in a small, crowded country like Japan."

These lines from Chapter 4, "A Common Master Plan," describe Mama's reluctance to use the partitionless toilets and connect her to the issues of Japanese identity traced in the stories of Papa, Woody, and Jeanne. Mama was born in Hawaii and does not struggle as much as Papa or Jeanne, who as noncitizen and citizen respectively, approach the Japanese-American identity problem from opposite circumstances. Yet Wakatsuki makes statements throughout the novel that remind us how much Mama also struggles to reconcile camp living with being Japanese. Two of the essentially Japanese values that Jeanne sees in Mama's selfless but proud character are cooperation and respect for privacy. The need to survive requires Mama to cooperate, but cooperating also means living in cramped quarters with blankets for walls and cardboard boxes for toilet partitions, which impinge on her privacy. Mama's frustration, especially with the toilets, underscores the incompatibility of these two traits in the context of camp life. Japanese cooperation went far in making life at Manzanar tolerable, but camp life itself was a constant insult to the inhabitants' concerns for privacy and dignity.

2. "When your mother and your father are having a fight, do you want them to kill each other? Or do you just want them to stop fighting?"

Papa's final question to the interrogator in Chapter 7, "Fort Lincoln: An Interview," is a striking metaphor for the difficult situation into which the war between the United States and Japan threw Japanese-American Issei. Most of the Issei, who left Japan for the greater opportunities offered in other countries, still had strong ties to their Japanese ancestry and saw Japan as their motherland. On the other hand, the United States was their adopted home, and even though they were not American citizens, they valued the opportunities that citizenship brought for their Nisei children. The war put the Issei in an impossible situation, for they could not declare loyalty to one country without jeopardizing their relationship to the other. Papa's question illustrates the difficulty that such things as the Loyalty Oath and the accusations of a military interrogator presented to him and other Issei.

QUOTATIONS

3. I smiled and sat down, suddenly aware of what being of Japanese ancestry was going to be like. I wouldn't be faced with physical attack, or with overt shows of hatred. Rather, I would be seen as someone foreign, or as someone other than American, or perhaps not be seen at all.

Jeanne comes to this realization about the true nature of prejudice in Chapter 20, "A Double Impulse," after her classmate Radine expresses surprise at Jeanne's ability to speak English. Before the war Jeanne rarely thinks about prejudice and does not even completely understand what it meant to be Japanese. Radine's reaction, however, forces her to recognize that hatred is not the dark force she imagined would be waiting for her when she left the camp, but rather a quiet undertone in everyday interactions. Radine's innocent comment is both a compliment and an insult, which makes Jeanne realize that prejudice is not the same as hatred and is not always malicious. Radine intends no harm, but her comment reflects prejudiced beliefs unwittingly inherited from her prejudiced mother, who later refuses to allow Jeanne to join the Girl Scout troop. While Jeanne does not hate Radine for viewing her as "someone other than American," she finds this perception of herself troubling and later connects the relocation of Japanese Americans with white America's inability to see the Japanese Americans as individual human beings. The discovery that this kind of prejudice can lie deeply hidden behind even innocent comments strips Jeanne of her naïveté and marks the beginning of her transition from child to adult.

QUOTATIONS

4.   I feel no malice toward this girl. I don't even envy her.
       Watching, I am simply emptied, and in the dream I want to
       cry out, because she is something I can never be, some
       possibility in my life that can never be fulfilled.

In Chapter 21, "The Girl of my Dreams," Jeanne explains the recurring dream she has had ever since witnessing Radine's sudden rise in popularity in high school. The girl in the dream is beautiful and blonde, admired by all, and represents Jeanne's desire for acceptance. Jeanne too wants to be admired, but she does not envy or hate the dream girl, just as she does not hate Radine for her successes. Jeanne's lack of envy and hate shows a remarkable maturity but also reflects the resignation and sadness of realizing that her dreams can never come true. She says her inability to achieve her goals makes her want to scream, but she does not cry out, which shows the extent to which she has accepted prejudice against those of Japanese ancestry as a simple fact of life. Even though she is hurt when her friends' parents exclude her, she never speaks out in protest; instead she blames herself for being different. As a teenager, she is less troubled by being treated differently than by having to watch others achieve what she cannot. It is not the dream girl herself that she resents, but the window that lets her look but not touch. This frustration leads to resignation, and the collective weight of five years of resignation eventually turns the image of her dream girl into a grim reminder that leaves her "emptied" of hope that things will ever change.

QUOTATIONS

5.   Papa's life ended at Manzanar.... Until this trip I had not
     been able to admit that my own life really began there.

Jeanne makes this observation when she sees her eleven-year-old
daughter walking through the ruins of Manzanar in Chapter 22,
"Ten Thousand Voices." Manzanar was the most important event
of Jeanne's life, and by tearing her family apart and forcing her to
face up to prejudice, it made her start her life from scratch. Manzanar wiped out her fondest memories of prewar family life and made
her look at herself in the light of postwar American prejudice. Yet,
until now, Jeanne never accepted the important role Manzanar played
in shaping her identity and had begun to erase the camp from her memory. Going back to the site brings her experiences back to life; she realizes that despite the difficulties she faced there, her time in Manzanar
made her stronger as a person, both during and after the war.

Jeanne contrasts her own experience at Manzanar with Papa's,
whose life, she says, ended there. After Manzanar, Papa's life
becomes such a struggle and is so unfulfilling that it can hardly be
called a life, and Jeanne hints that it was Manzanar that weakened
him and left him unable to cope with returning. Upon leaving the
camp, Papa continues to drink himself to death, remains dependent
on Mama and Woody because he is too proud to take a menial job,
and desperately clings to empty hopes such as his doomed housing
project. He drives a permanent wedge between himself and Jeanne,
and ceases to be an important part of Jeanne's story. Jeanne grows
up looking up to Papa, but with the virtual ending of his life in Manzanar, she must begin a new life with a new outlook.

QUOTATIONS

KEY FACTS

FULL TITLE
Farewell to Manzanar

AUTHOR
Jeanne Wakatsuki Houston

TYPE OF WORK
Nonfiction

GENRE
Historical memoir; bildungsroman, or coming-of-age story

LANGUAGE
English

TIME AND PLACE WRITTEN
1972–1973; Santa Cruz, California

DATE OF FIRST PUBLICATION
1973

PUBLISHER
San Francisco Book Company / Houghton Mifflin

NARRATOR
Jeanne Wakatsuki Houston

POINT OF VIEW
The narrator speaks in the first person and describes the events and characters as she herself witnessed them, with the exception of the chapters "Fort Lincoln: An Interview," "The Reservoir Shack: An Aside," and "Ka-ke, Near Hiroshima: April, 1946," where she switches to third person to describe the experiences of Papa, Kaz, and Woody respectively.

TONE
Houston is observational throughout much of the novel, relating her memories of her experiences and emotions. Toward the end of the work, when Houston revisits Manzanar to confront her past, her narrative becomes nostalgic and less straightforward.

TENSE
Houston tells the story primarily in the past tense, with
occasional shifts to reflect her thoughts and feelings as she writes.

SETTING (TIME)
December 1942–April 1972

SETTING (PLACE)
The California cities of Long Beach, Los Angeles, Manzanar, and
San Jose

PROTAGONIST
Jeanne Wakatsuki Houston

MAJOR CONFLICT
Jeanne struggles to gain acceptance in white American society
and to find her own identity as a Japanese-American woman.

RISING ACTION
After being forced to leave the Manzanar Relocation Camp, the
Wakatsukis try to reintegrate themselves into American society,
but Jeanne's attempts to gain acceptance at school are blocked by
the unspoken prejudice of her classmates and teachers in Long
Beach.

CLIMAX
Jeanne's high school in San Jose elects her carnival queen, but
Papa accuses her of flaunting her sexuality and trying to be
American.

FALLING ACTION
Jeanne conforms to Papa's wishes and wears a conservative dress
for the coronation ceremony, but the crowd's murmuring makes
her realize that neither the exotic nor the conservative versions of
herself represent her true identity.

THEMES
Internment's destruction of family life; the everyday nature of
prejudice; the difficulty of understanding one's identity

MOTIFS
Displacement; Americana

SYMBOLS
Stones; Jeanne's dream

FORESHADOWING

The sardine fleet's slow return to the harbor foreshadows the news of the attack on Pearl Harbor; Papa's burning of his flag and documents foreshadows his arrest and interrogation as a suspected spy.

KEY FACTS

STUDY QUESTIONS & ESSAY TOPICS

STUDY QUESTIONS

1. *Much of* FAREWELL TO MANZANAR *deals with Jeanne's struggle to discover her identity. How does her Japanese identity conflict with her American identity? How does her experience with prejudice help her to reconcile the two?*

In the early part of the work, Jeanne does not define herself much at all, and simply describes what she sees. The way that she describes the world around her, however, makes it clear that she associates herself much more with American culture than with Japanese culture. She has fond memories of her big frame house in the non-Japanese neighborhood of Ocean Park and remembers her kind white schoolteacher who cried when the Wakatsukis left. In fact, when Mama finally moves the family to a Japanese ghetto on Terminal Island, Jeanne reveals that it is the first time she has ever lived among other Japanese people. That Asian faces frighten her and that she thinks of the Japanese community as a foreign country show that she does not really think of herself as Japanese.

Jeanne's inability to connect with her culture continues at Manzanar, and as she tries to find ways to spend her free time, she almost always gravitates to non-Japanese pursuits such as baton twirling, the Glee Club, and even Catholicism. One of the few Japanese activities she does try, traditional Japanese *odori* dancing, ends in failure because Jeanne cannot understand the teacher's old dialect and mysterious ways. Language proves a barrier, but her problems in connecting to her heritage are more the result of her having never visited Japan and thus not understanding Japanese culture. To Jeanne, anything traditionally Japanese looks alien, and no seven-year-old can enjoy something that is frightening and confusing. Jeanne does share certain attitudes with all of the Japanese at Manzanar, such as the revulsion at eating apricots over rice, but she does not connect with them about Japanese culture in any meaningful way.

Jeanne comes to understand Japanese people and customs during her time at Manzanar, but she does not understand how her Japanese ancestry makes her different until she returns to Long Beach after the war. Living in an ethnically mixed neighborhood, she is unable to avoid the fact that she is different, and she begins to see all of the prejudices to which she was earlier blind. Before Manzanar, Jeanne would have been just as perplexed as she is now by Radine's surprise at her natural English fluency, but she probably would not have interpreted it as prejudice. Now, however, after preparing herself in camp for the hatred she expects to experience outside, Jeanne is sensitive to the unspoken, hidden forms of prejudice that existed even before the war. The discovery of this anti-Japanese prejudice makes Jeanne begin to think about her ancestry. At first she tries to deny her heritage by acting like her white schoolmates, but she eventually realizes that just as her experiences at Manzanar play a crucial role in shaping her life, so her Japanese heritage forms a crucial part of her identity.

2.   *What is the role of non-Japanese characters in Wakatsuki's memoir?*

There are very few non-Japanese characters in *Farewell to Manzanar*, and they play a limited and specific role in the story. Often, these characters serve to make a point about Jeanne or how she sees the world around her. Wakatsuki rarely, if ever, uses them to condemn white society or prejudice in general. Her schoolteachers—before, during, and after her time at Manzanar—are invariably non-Japanese, but Wakatsuki uses the fact that some are nurturing while others are fearful and prejudiced to show that race alone cannot define a person. Not all whites are as small-minded as the teachers at San Jose who try to prevent her from becoming carnival queen, just as not all Japanese were responsible for the attack on Pearl Harbor.

Although tolerance is an important aspect of the work, the non-Japanese characters often appear faceless and distant in order to clarify the true conflict in the work. *Farewell to Manzanar* speaks more deeply and effectively about acceptance of self, and Jeanne's struggle with herself shows us that before one can ever hope to confront prejudice, he or she must come to terms with himself or herself. Throughout much of the memoir, Jeanne has an uncertain, sometimes negative tone about being Japanese, and she is not able to feel whole as a person until the carnival queen ceremony, at which she finally begins to accept herself as neither essentially American nor entirely exotic. The non-Japanese characters do not need to be developed, because even in the cases of Leonard Rodriguez and Radine, they are present in the work only as signposts marking Jeanne's growing knowledge of herself and her complex identity.

3.   *Upon returning from Manzanar, Jeanne finds that the hatred she must face is very different from the "dark cloud" she imagined would descend on her. What are the different forms of hatred depicted in* FAREWELL TO MANZANAR, *and how do they manifest themselves?*

Wakatsuki explores prejudice through her experiences with whites before and after the war as well as through her experiences among Japanese Americans at Manzanar. Early on, even in the description of the relocation itself, Wakatsuki leaves ethnic prejudice largely undeveloped, though she plants the idea of such prejudice through characters such as the unscrupulous secondhand dealer who tries to cheat Mama and the cold teacher in Boyle Heights. Before Manzanar, the prejudice that does surface is undefined and confusing, much as it must have been for young Jeanne. In fact, Wakatsuki does not directly address the idea of hatred until her family's arrival at Manzanar, where hatred and fighting, suspicions and accusations occur among the Japanese themselves. Wakatsuki uses events such as the beating of Fred Tayama and the ensuing December Riots to show that a group cannot address the greater issue of prejudice until it deals with internal conflicts.

The violent hatred Jeanne fears so much before leaving the camp differs drastically from the deep but subtle prejudice she eventually encounters in Long Beach. She imagines a "dark cloud" of hatred but finds only an ill-defined haze. There are no lynchings, no beatings; much of the prejudice she encounters is indirect, unspoken, or hidden. Her most open encounter is Radine's innocent surprise at Jeanne's ability to speak English. But she realizes that Radine is conditioned to think Japanese people cannot speak English and that the comment represents a much wider and more intangible prejudice. Hatred, as Wakatsuki depicts it in the latter half of the memoir, is not an open, direct threat, but a hidden force that pervades everything from the Girl Scouts to the choice of the high school band's majorette. This is a much more dangerous form of hatred because it is difficult to identify, difficult to prove, and, as Wakatsuki's experiences testify, almost impossible to fight alone.

Suggested Essay Topics

1. There are three semifictional chapters in FAREWELL TO MANZANAR. Why does Wakatsuki combine fictionalized elements with the nonfiction of a memoir?

2. Discuss the generation gap between Issei immigrants and their Nisei children. How are they different? What characteristics do they share?

3. Wakatsuki never seems bitter about her experience in Manzanar and never directly condemns the relocation policy. Why does she choose not to pass judgment?

4. How does Jeanne's view of Japanese Americans change throughout the work?

5. How does Wakatsuki develop Papa as a tragic figure? Why does she make him so central to her story?

6. What are the chief differences between Woody and Papa? How are they similar?

7. Wakatsuki gives almost no information about the war in the course of the memoir. Why does she choose to leave the war out of her story for the most part?

REVIEW & RESOURCES

QUIZ

1. What does Jeanne imagine hatred looks like?

    A. A heavy stone
    B. A dark cloud
    C. A puff of smoke
    D. A dense fog

2. What aspect of camp life does Mama find particularly hard to tolerate?

    A. The poor food
    B. The lack of warm clothing
    C. The long lines for the shower
    D. Toilets without partitions

3. To what social class in Japan does Papa's family belong?

    A. Farmers
    B. Merchants
    C. Samurai
    D. Nobility

4. What was the center of Wakatsuki family life before the war?

    A. Samurai sword fights
    B. Papa reading the newspaper aloud
    C. Saying farewell to the departing fishing boats
    D. Meals around the wooden table

5. What Japanese word means both "dog" and "collaborator"?

    A. *eno*
    B. *inu*
    C. *ono*
    D. *ani*

6. What does Kiyo do to stop Papa from striking Mama?

    A. He breaks Mama's china.
    B. He calls the camp police.
    C. He punches Papa in the face.
    D. He lets Papa strike him instead.

7. What do the Wakatsukis discover when they wake up the first morning in camp?

    A. Their barracks is covered in sand.
    B. Papa has returned.
    C. Their belongings have been stolen.
    D. Woody has prepared breakfast in bed.

8. Of what does the interrogator accuse Papa?

    A. Not giving the names of all of his children
    B. Supplying oil to a Japanese submarine
    C. Selling secrets to the Japanese military
    D. Bombing Pearl Harbor

9. What is the name of Bill's band?

    A. The Jitterbugs
    B. The Fenced-in Five
    C. The Bigtime Brass
    D. The Jive Bombers

10. What does the girl of Jeanne's dream look like?

    A. A dark exotic beauty
    B. A blonde prom queen
    C. A character from *Gone with the Wind*
    D. Exactly like Jeanne

11. What impresses Woody most about Aunt Toyo?

    A. Her dignity
    B. That she survived the bombing of Hiroshima
    C. The meal she serves him
    D. Her ability to speak English

12. Why did Papa leave Japan?

  A. He found a cheap ticket
  B. He couldn't find a job in Japan
  C. He was ashamed of his family
  D. His family made him leave

13. What position in the high school band is Jeanne excluded from because she is Japanese?

  A. Song girl
  B. Majorette
  C. Mascot
  D. Cheerleader

14. Where does Jeanne watch her parents make up after a long period of arguments?

  A. In the firebreak
  B. In the car on the way to Long Beach
  C. On the steps of their barracks
  D. In the bedroom

15. Where does Jeanne say her life began?

  A. Inglewood, California
  B. Hiroshima, Japan
  C. Terminal Island
  D. Manzanar

16. What is the cause of the December Riot?

  A. The beating of Fred Tayama
  B. The arrest of the men who beat up Fred Tayama
  C. The shooting of two Japanese men who beat up Fred Tayama
  D. The beating of two Japanese men who shot Fred Tayama

REVIEW & RESOURCES

17. Whose Supreme Court case results in the closing of the camps?

    A. Gordon Hirabayashi's
    B. Fred Korematsu's
    C. Woody Wakatsuki's
    D. Mitsue Endo's

18. What memory of Papa does Jeanne recall during her visit to Manzanar?

    A. Papa striking Mama with his cane
    B. Papa standing on the deck of his fishing boat
    C. Papa driving crazily through camp in his new car
    D. Papa carving a pig at an anniversary party

19. What is the subject of the Japanese anthem, *Kimi ga yo*?

    A. The glory of the emperor
    B. The endurance of stones
    C. The length of the year
    D. The wetness of moss

20. What is Jeanne's first experience with prejudice after returning from Manzanar?

    A. Her classmates' surprise at her ability to speak English
    B. An old woman spits on her
    C. A bathroom sign that says "whites only"
    D. A schoolyard bully

21. How long did Jeanne stay at Manzanar?

    A. Six months
    B. One year
    C. Two years
    D. Three years

22. What does Jeanne hear when she visits the site of the Manzanar camp in 1972?

   A. Voices
   B. Birds
   C. Cars from the highway
   D. Nothing

23. What photograph appears in the final edition of the Manzanar High School yearbook?

   A. A watchtower with searchlights
   B. An old woman on a path with her dog
   C. A massive stone covered in thick moss
   D. A hand squeezing pliers on a barbed-wire fence

24. What does Mama do when the secondhand dealer offers her too little money for her china?

   A. She tries to attack him
   B. She breaks her china
   C. She accepts his offer because she is poor
   D. She decides to sell her china for more money in Los Angeles

25. How does Jeanne dress for the carnival queen election assembly?

   A. In a strapless prom dress
   B. In a conservative dress
   C. In an exotic sarong
   D. In military fatigues

ANSWER KEY:

1: B; 2: D; 3: C; 4: D; 5: B; 6: C; 7: A; 8: B; 9: D; 10: B; 11: A; 12: C; 13: A; 14: A; 15: D; 16: D; 17: D; 18: C; 19: C; 20: A; 21: D; 22: A; 23: D; 24: B; 25: C

SUGGESTIONS FOR FURTHER READING

BALLARD, J. G. *Empire of the Sun.* New York: Simon & Schuster, 1984.

DANIELS, ROGER, SANDRA TAYLOR, and HARRY KITANO, eds. *Japanese Americans: From Relocation to Redress.* Seattle: University of Washington Press, 1994.

HARTH, ERICA, ed. *Last Witnesses: Reflections on the Wartime Internment of Japanese Americans.* New York: Palgrave, 2001.

HIGASHIDE, SEIICHI. *Adios to Tears: The Memoirs of a Japanese-Peruvian Internee in U.S. Concentration Camps.* Seattle: University of Washington Press, 2000.

HILL, KIMI KODANI, ed. *Topaz Moon: Chiura Obata's Art of the Internment.* Berkeley: Heydey Books, 2000.

KIYAMA, HENRY. *The Four Immigrants Manga: A Japanese Experience in San Francisco, 1904–1922.* Berkeley, California: Stone Bridge Press, 1998.

OKUBO, MINE. *Citizen 13660.* Seattle: University of Washington Press, 1983.

STANLEY, JERRY. *I am an American: A True Story of Japanese Internment.* New York: Crown, 1994.

UCHIDA, YOSHIKO. *Desert Exile: The Uprooting of a Japanese-American Family.* Seattle: University of Washington Press, 1984.

WAKATSUKI HOUSTON, JEANNE. *Beyond Manzanar: Views of Asian American Womanhood.* Santa Barbara, California: Capra Press, 1985.

YAMAMOTO, HISAYE. *Seventeen Syllables and Other Stories.* New Brunswick, New Jersey: Rutgers University Press, 1998.

REVIEW & RESOURCES

SPARKNOTES TEST PREPARATION GUIDES

The SparkNotes team figured it was time to cut standardized tests down to size. We've studied the tests for you, so that SparkNotes test prep guides are:

Smarter
Packed with critical-thinking skills and test-
taking strategies that will improve your score.

Better
Fully up to date, covering all new features of the tests,
with study tips on every type of question.

Faster
Our books cover exactly what you need to
know for the test. No more, no less.

SparkNotes Literature Guides